THE G[...]
TASTE GUIDE:
JERSEY

JULIA HUNT

Private Table Press

Published by

Private Table Press

1st Edition 2011

Copyright © 2011 by Julia Hunt

All photos unless stated © 2011 by Victoria Stewart

Book design by Matt Swann
21stbookdesign.blogspot.com

All rights reserved. No part of this publication may be reproduced in any form without the written consent of the copyright owner.

The publisher has done its best to ensure the accuracy and completeness of this guide. However, the publisher accepts no responsibility for any loss, injury, or inconvenience sustained as a result of information or advice in this guide.

CONTENTS

INTRODUCTION 4
ABOUT JERSEY 7
JERSEY PRODUCE 9

FINE DINING 12

BISTROS AND BRASSERIES 26

INFORMAL DINING 38

SEAFOOD 48

MEDITERRANEAN 56

ASIAN 64

GRILLS 68

PUB DINING 72

CAFES 78

LOCATIONS AND TRAVEL 88
FOOD EVENTS 90
GETTING TO JERSEY 91
TRAVEL ON THE ISLAND 93

PHOTOGRAPH CREDITS 94

AUTHOR INFORMATION 96

INTRODUCTION

From Michelin starred meals to simple snacks, Jersey has wonderful food for all appetites and occasions. With over 200 restaurants in an area less than nine miles by five, visitors and residents alike have plenty of choice.

The Good Taste Guide: Jersey is the only known food guide to the island where restaurants cannot pay to be included and do not have any control over what is written. All establishments are chosen on the merit of what they offer, bringing together 50 of the best places to eat at the moment across a range of cuisines for all budgets.

Establishments are listed according to style of cuisine so if you're seeking seafood or have carnivorous cravings, fancy fine dining or would just like to go to a gastro-pub, you can easily target the right places. Our independent reviews give a flavour for what restaurants are really like for paying customers as each place has been visited by an undercover diner. The guide does not accept hospitality from restaurants or rely on any advertising from them, ensuring total impartiality.

Restaurants are selected on grounds of quality – both of the food and the overall experience. No matter how good a chef, if service is so slow a snail could crawl away before it is cooked, why should you spend your money there? A good meal does not have to be expensive; however, it is unlikely to be cheap. Fresh food prepared on site will naturally cost more than mass-produced items which could be reheated by a monkey with a microwave. Jersey has an abundance of local produce which provides a fabulous framework for a talented chef.

The ethos of The Good Taste Guides is selecting places where discerning diners will enjoy eating, that we have tested and can happily recommend to others who appreciate good food. Whether you're planning a romantic dinner by the beach, wanting somewhere for a business lunch in town or just hoping to find a pleasant spot for a family meal in the countryside, The Good Taste Guides are designed to help you discover somewhere which suits your requirements.

Eating out in Jersey is no more expensive than eating out in the UK and is generally less than comparable meals in France. For example, a three-course dinner at one of the island's Michelin starred restaurants

costs about £60 per head, food only, a relative bargain when similar places on the continent can charge that much for one dish. Although restaurants in Jersey face higher food costs for imported items and have high labour costs this is tempered by a business friendly infrastructure. In addition there is no VAT in Jersey, just a Goods and Service Tax (GST) of 5%.

We hope you enjoy this first edition of The Good Taste Guides. We welcome your feedback and suggestions can be made through our website, www.goodtasteguides.com

ABOUT JERSEY

The largest of the Channel Islands, Jersey is the most southerly part of the British Isles. Just 14 miles from the Normandy coast, yet over 100 miles from English ports, Jersey is a Crown Dependency. Although less than an hour by boat from Guernsey, the two islands are totally separate entities with different governments, flags and infrastructures.

With over 92,000 inhabitants, Jersey is one of the most densely populated parts of Europe, yet, thanks to tight planning laws and housing regulations, much of the island remains unspoilt, with a pattern of small fields and narrow lanes which haven't changed much in centuries. Jersey's economy is mainly based on finance, tourism and agriculture; however, don't expect to see any skyscrapers; offices are more likely to be tucked away in picturesque granite cottages.

Occupied by the Nazis during World War Two, Jersey's coastline displays remnants of this period and the work slave labourers and Jersey men were forced to do. Most of the south and west coastline is ringed with a sea wall, built as part of the Atlantic Defence, while former gun turrets have been converted into fish hatcheries, deckchair stores or cafes. Anyone interested in finding out more about the occupation should visit Jersey War Tunnels, a museum set in the Germans' secret underground hospital.

Martello towers are another architectural reminder of Jersey's military history. These turrets were built in the 18th century to defend the island against a French invasion. Some, like the Seymour Tower, between St Helier and Gorey, are only accessible at low tide, when Jersey's landmass can extend over two miles from the shore.

As well as a number of forts, such as the 16th century St Aubin's Fort, now used as a water sports centre, Jersey has three castles. Built during the reign of Elizabeth I, Elizabeth Castle, St Helier, and the earlier Mont Orgueil, Gorey are in good condition, while the 14th century Grosnez Castle, near Plemont, is in ruins.

Opposite top: High tide at St Aubin's Harbour
Opposite bottom: Elizabeth Castle, St Helier

JERSEY PRODUCE

Palm-tree lined promenades are a good indication of Jersey's climate. While temperatures can reach 25C in the summer, winters are generally mild and frost and snow are rare. A moderate amount of rain helps create a good environment for crops and with more than 100 items grown in 30,000 vergées (about 15,000 acres) of fields, glass houses or poly-tunnels, if you're happy eating what is in season you can enjoy local food all year.

Jersey's best known crop is potatoes and Jersey Royals are the only product outside the European Union to gain an Appellation d' Origine Contrôlée status. Grown on steep slopes called côtils, and fertilised with vraic, as seaweed is known in Jèrriais, the season runs from April to July. Up to 1,500 tons a day are harvested for export, although you can thankfully still find plenty on the island and virtually all spring or summer menus feature Jersey Royals.

Although Jersey Royals take up more than half the island's agricultural land, there is still a little diversity. Organic and non-organic fruit and vegetables are grown for local consumption and export. Crops of note include asparagus, from April to June, purple sprouting broccoli from December to April and strawberries from May to September. Jersey also grows excellent watercress, which is sold on the island in large bunches which last much longer than standard bagged leaves.

A good way of finding out what is in season is to walk past roadside stalls which farmers and keen gardeners fill with whatever they have in abundance. Popular stalls include Joe Freire for strawberries; Didier Hellio for vegetables and L'Etacq for Jersey Royals. There are also a number of farm shops selling a broader range of local produce which are ideal if you are self-catering or preparing a beach picnic. Some of the larger ones include Holme Grown, Grouville; Farm Fresh Organics, St Lawrence; Vermont Farm, St Brelade and Rondels, Trinity.

Restaurants using certified local produce may display a Genuine Jersey logo on their menus. This red sign indicates the producer is a member of the Genuine Jersey Products Association, which is usually a good indication of quality.

FISH AND SEAFOOD

Hand-dived scallops, spider crabs and European lobsters are some of the delicacies found in Jersey's waters. More than 1,200 tons of shellfish are landed each year, in addition to over 1,000 tons of oysters and over 200 tons of Bouchot mussels which are cultivated by the Jersey Oyster Company and La Rocque Fisheries in Royal Grouville Bay. Noisette Oysters, which are served in places like The Oyster Box, are particular to Jersey and strong tidal currents and low density cultivation help create a quality product which is particularly popular in France. Caught in pots, Jersey lobsters are served in restaurants across the island and the area is set to be only the second lobster fishing zone in the world to be certified by the Marine Stewardship Council.

Less than one ton of wet fish is landed in Jersey for every 10 tons of shellfish and this small scale ensures local waters are not over-fished. Restaurants such as Jersey Pottery, which take fish from Genuine Jersey member Kevin Holden, use everything landed so very little is thrown back. Local fish include sea bass, available from May to November, mackerel from April to November and black bream from May to September. Brill and sole are found all year, as is turbot, which is farmed in a converted WW2 gun turret near St Catherine's.

MEAT

With their luscious long lashes and huge brown eyes it is difficult to imagine eating a Jersey cow, however, with island cattle, beef is actually a tasty by-product of the dairy herds. In order to produce milk, cows need to have a calf, and while females join the herd, some of the males are raised to form Jersey Beef, a tender, well marbled meat served in restaurants such as Tides at The Somerville, or more casually as burgers at The Hungry Man. A number of farms are also involved in a new breeding initiative using Jersey dairy cows and Aberdeen Angus beef cows, offering something to look out for on menus in 2012.

Island farmers also produce small quantities of lamb and pork. John Hackett's outdoor reared pork can be found in restaurants such as La Cantina in the form of Luganega sausages.

DAIRY

Jersey cows produce milk with 20% more calcium and 18% more protein than other dairy breeds. However, at 6% fat, many people find this too creamy for everyday consumption so this is now sold in 500ml yellow cartons labelled Full Cream Milk. The green cartons of Fat Reduced milk contain 3% fat, slightly less than UK Standard Milk while blue cartons of 1% Fat Milk are close to Semi-Skimmed. Jersey Dairy takes milk from 27 island farms which it uses for a range of yoghurts, creams and ice cream in delectable flavours like lemon meringue or apple and cinnamon, which you will find in many beachside cafes. Cheese is not a traditional Jersey product, however, Jersey Dairy make a mature cheddar and Classic Herd have an award winning range of soft cheeses such as Jersey Brie, Camembert and Nouveau as well as the rather moreish Golden Blue, well worth sampling if you spot it on a cheeseboard.

CIDER, BEER AND WINE

In the early 19th century apples were Jersey's biggest cash crop, producing hundreds of thousands of gallons of cider a year for export to the UK. Walking along Green Lanes you can still see raised edges to fields, designed to shelter the trees. Some orchards have been replanted and people like Richard Matlock at La Robeline Cider produce a traditional sparkling cider which is sold at farm markets, in supermarkets and on tap in Liberation Group pubs. Jersey Brewery makes its own beers on the island including the CAMRA award-winning Liberation Ale and the 130-year-old Mary Ann bitter, while La Mare Vineyard has been growing grapes since the 1970s, and now produces a range of red, white, pink and sparkling wines along with fruit liqueurs.

FINE DINING

SUMA'S

Gorey Hill, Gorey, St Martin | 01534 853291 | www.sumasrestaurant.com

Opening Times: Monday-Friday noon-2.30pm, 6-10pm; Saturday 9-11am, noon-2.30pm, 6-10pm; Sunday 9-11am, noon-4pm

Set Menus: Lunch Monday-Saturday, dinner Monday-Thursday and early dinner Friday-Saturday, two courses £17, three courses £19.50. Sunday lunch two courses £18.50, three courses £22.50

Average price two-course à la carte meal for one (excluding drinks): £30

House Wine Bottle: £14; **Glass:** £4

Car Parking: Opposite restaurant

Unassuming from the back, yet with outstanding views of Gorey Harbour to the front, Suma's is the perfect example of allowing quality to speak for itself. Owned by a branch of the family behind Longueville Manor, Suma's standards are high, although in a much more casual way. It's jeans rather than black tie, the bar is a simple counter of bottles, the walls are white-washed bricks, and the menu is kinder on your waistline and wallet. The chef, Daniel Ward, champions local produce such as oysters from Grouville Bay, just beyond the balcony, and turbot from St Catherine's just around the corner. Bread is handmade and great companions with starters like home-cured salmon or squid with a tomato and chorizo compote. Mains are a feast for fish-lovers with specials like John Dory, pan fried on a rack of local asparagus with a colourful, fresh mango salsa, while meat-eaters can enjoy a good selection of Angus beef with a red onion and chicken liver mille-feuille, duck with juniper sauce or perhaps venison with vanilla poached pears. Puddings, like the chocolate trio, with a tiramisu style pave, a warm chocolate fondant with a gooey white chocolate middle and a chilli flecked chocolate sorbet, are so beautifully presented you could hang them on the wall if they didn't taste so good.

Highlight: Fresh flavoursome food from people who are passionate about it

OCEAN RESTAURANT

The Atlantic Hotel,
Le Mont de la Pulente,
St Brelade, JE3 8HE
01534 744101
www.theatlantichotel.com

Opening Times:
Monday-Sunday 12.30-2.30pm;
7-10pm

Set Menus: Three-course
Table d'hôte £50;
three-course à la carte £60;
Seven-course Tasting menu £75

House Wine Bottle: £23; **Glass:** £6 | **Car Parking:** On site

Michelin Star cooking, sea views and the finest ingredients combine at Ocean. Head Chef Mark Jordan creates dishes which are as fresh and elegant as the setting, in a luxury hotel on the top of cliffs overlooking the Atlantic. The restaurant has a New England feel with white shutters and an azure and sand decor, however, the cuisine is inspired as much by island produce as by the chef's training with Keith Floyd and Jean-Christophe Novelli. Starters include a dainty portion of langoustine, sandwiched between a slice of crispy bacon and a layer of tender anise flavoured pork belly, and pan-fried foie gras, deliciously offset with caramelised apples. Fish features predominantly with the mains and naturally includes perfectly cooked line caught Jersey bass along with halibut, firm fleshed with a slightly sweet sear on top of asparagus and hot cheese gnocchi, while a shot glass of pea puree adds another layer of flavours. Desserts are extravagant exhibitions along a theme. The Raspberry; smooth raspberry sorbet and a tower of spun sugar, raspberries and pistachio cream, is as delightful to taste as to admire. Naturally, apple crumble is not nearly as simple as it sounds, with deconstructed components of toffee apple and pastry transforming a humble pudding into a Jacques Derrida of desserts.

Highlight: Excellent combinations of flavours which appeal on visual and gastronomic levels

BOHEMIA

The Club Hotel and Spa, Green Street, St Helier, JE2 4UH
01534 876500 | www.bohemiajersey.com

Opening Times: Monday-Saturday noon-2.30pm; 6.30-10pm

Set Menus: Two-course lunch £18.50, three courses £21.50; Three-course dinner £55

House Wine Bottle: £14; **Glass:** £3.25 | **Car Parking:** Green Street

Boasting a Michelin Star since 2005, and four AA rosettes, Bohemia sets the tone for fine dining in St Helier. Located on the ground floor of the Club and Spa Hotel, the restaurant is a chic combination of stone tiles, tobacco-leather chairs and walnut veneered walls. After opening with an amuse bouche such as the frozen martini, a refreshing scoop of vodka sorbet saltily offset with a green olive, and fortifying yourself with delicious homemade bread your taste buds are suitably tantalised. Dishes exhibit local produce like line-caught sea bass, hand-dived scallops and Jersey Royals although flavours can sometimes challenge rather than simply compliment ingredients. For example, a sweet cube of pork belly is juxtaposed with powerful braised pig's cheek, while tuna sashimi has to stand up to cucumber sorbet and vanilla dressing. However, with a cook book and TV show behind him, Chef Shaun Rankin can't rest on his still scrumptious treacle tart.

Highlight: Exquisitely presented food in a chic cadre

SIROCCO

The Royal Yacht Hotel | 01534 720511
www.theroyalyacht.com

Opening Times: Monday-Saturday 7-10pm; Sunday 12.30-3pm, 7-10pm

Set Menus: Three-course Sunday lunch £19; three-course Table d'Hôte £25; Tasting menu £67

Average price two-course à la carte meal for one (excluding drinks): £36

House Wine Bottle: £16.50; **Glass:** £3.95 | **Car Parking:** The Esplanade

On the first floor of the Royal Yacht Hotel, a glass wall floods Sirocco with light and offers lovely views over the marina, making the modern room pleasant for evening meals or Sunday lunch. Large round tables make this suitable for groups who can start the night on the terrace and finish in the nightclub below. The table d'hôte menu, with a selection of dishes like carpaccio of beef with delicate quails eggs salad or a moist roasted breast of guinea fowl with fondant potatoes and rich Madeira jus, offers good value. If you upscale, there's a seven-course tasting menu with delicacies like foie gras with spiced cherries, wild turbot with caviar and loin of lamb with caramelised sweetbreads. The à la carte menu is somewhere in between featuring a selection of quality produce, some of which, like the steak and the Crêpe Suzette are flambéed by the professional waiters at your table.

Highlight: Plush place for a glamorous night out

CHATEAU LA CHAIRE

La Vallee de Rozel, St Martin, JE3 6AJ
01534 863354 | www.chateau-la-chaire.co.uk

Opening Times: Monday-Sunday noon-2pm, 7-9pm and from 10.30am for coffee and cakes and 2.30-5pm for afternoon tea

Set Menus: Three-course lunch Monday-Saturday £14.95; Sunday lunch £17.95; six-course dinner £32.95

House Wine Bottle: £18.95; **Glass:** £4.75 | **Car Parking:** On site

The oak panelled dining room of Chateau La Chaire hotel is a restaurant for residents and visitors alike. Elegant yet cosy, the room is perfect for a romantic dinner in winter, while the conservatory and wisteria edged terrace are wonderful for lunch or summer evenings. Cooking is refined Mediterranean served by friendly yet efficient waiters. Open with salmon cannelloni, two tubes of smoked fish generously stuffed with picked chancre crab, or scallops, a substantial dish of four king scallops, seared in pancetta. Mains like monkfish, a line of firm medallions set on moist saffron risotto, or sea bass, a crisp fillet served with crab filled potato croquettes, are satisfying and allow the full flavour of the fish to come through. What with an amuse-bouche such as crab in confit tomato and a scoop of bitter citrus sorbet, you might not have room for pudding, although the coffee pannacotta, served in a small cup, with langue de chat biscuits, is a creamy compromise worth making before retiring to the elaborate rococo drawing room for mint tea and petit-fours. Once home to Victorian horticulturalist Samuel Curtis, the gardens are delightful for a post-dinner stroll.

Highlight: A traditional dining experience in a beautiful setting

TIDES

The Somerville Hotel
01534 741226
www.dolanhotels.com/
the-somerville-hotel

Opening Times: Monday-Sunday 12.30-1.45pm, 7-8.45pm

Set menus: Summer Lobster Special with salad, pudding and coffee, £24.75

Average price two-course à la carte meal for one (excluding drinks): £28

House Wine Bottle: £18; **Glass:** £4.80

Car Parking: On site

On the hillside above St Aubins, The Somerville Hotel is one of the most distinct buildings on Jersey's south coast. The interior of the hotel is just as elegant as its exterior, with a fresh classic decor which works well at night, while at lunchtime, or early evening, large windows reveal fabulous sea views. With two AA rosettes, Tides offers a good selection of modern French cuisine, using local Jersey produce. Typical dishes include a tartlet of Jersey crab, served with cucumber crème-fraîche, a salad of partridge with foie gras, or a duo of roast and braised lamb with roasted squash and parsnips. Puddings are temptingly imaginative, with items like a Jersey black butter soufflé with honey crème anglaise or apple crème brûlée with jelly and sorbet, offering an indulgent finale. In addition to the regular wine list, a number of grand cru Bordeaux and Burgundies are also available to pre-order.

Highlight: Elegant food, wine and views make it easy to indulge

TASSILI

Grand Jersey, Esplanade, St Helier, JE2 3QA
01534 722301 | www.grandjersey.com

Opening Times: Tuesday-Saturday 7-10pm

Set Menus: Three courses £49; six-course tasting menu £67, nine-course surprise menu £87

House Wine Bottle: £16.95; **Glass:** £3.25

Car Parking: On site or The Esplanade

Developed under Albert Roux, Tassili already has three AA Rosettes, and is pushing for a Michelin star. With just nine tables, the black and pink dining room is a cocoon in the Grand Jersey which lends itself to special occasions for small groups or romantic meals. The set menus feature local and seasonal ingredients such as Jersey scallops, line-caught sea bass, foraged wild berries or island samphire. Head chef Richard Allen lifts sympathetic combinations with imaginative additions; lemon sole and mussel fricassée are joined by poached grapes; scallops and confit pork belly sit alongside roasted cèpes; while warm Armagnac tart shares the stage with salted caramel pudding and sweet raisin ice cream. Thoroughly modern, the food is artistically presented yet is resolutely pleasurable rather than pretentious. Service is swift and the Champagne Bar is a pleasant spot to enjoy an aperitif if you end up waiting for your table.

Highlight: Sophisticated food out to impress

LONGUEVILLE MANOR

Longueville Road, St Saviour, JE2 7WF
01534 725501 | www.longuevillemanor.com

Opening Times: Monday-Sunday 12.30-2pm; 7pm-10pm

Set Menus: Lunch two courses £20, three courses £25, Sunday lunch £35;
Dinner two courses £47.50, three courses £55;
seven-course Discovery menu £75

Average price two-course à la carte meal for one (excluding drinks): £47

House Wine Price Bottle: £20; **Glass:** £5

Car Parking: On site

With its sweeping driveway and elegant facade, Longueville Manor is one of Jersey's most beautiful hotels. The country house experience starts with an aperitif in one of the sitting rooms where giant olives and home-made bread sticks are a perfect accompaniment for a flute of Champagne or even a shot of vodka and freshly squeezed juice. At your table, in the panelled Oak Room or brighter Garden Room, well choreographed waiters start the show with an amuse-bouche, such as hot fish croquettes served on a slate. Menus include sophisticated dishes made with prime ingredients like hand-dived scallops with garden-grown asparagus; fillet of beef with an exquisitely rich oxtail ravioli; or turbot with Champagne beurre blanc and ginger. Puddings are a perfect finale showcasing the artistry of the chef, Andrew Baird. Delights include a dark chocolate and pistachio terrine with candied pineapple or the intriguing Pandora's Box, a chocolate bomb detonated at the table with warm banana cream.

Highlight: Exemplary food and service in a luxurious environment

BISTROS AND BRASSERIES

GREEN ISLAND RESTAURANT

Green Island, St Clement, Jersey, JE2 6LS
01534 857 787 | www.greenisland.je

Opening Times: Tuesday-Saturday noon-2.30pm, 6.45-9.30pm; Sunday noon-2.30pm

Set Menus: Three-course dinner, £21.50, Tuesday-Thursday. Two-course lunch £15.95, three courses £18

Average price two-course à la carte meal for one (excluding drinks): £25

House Wine Bottle: £14.95; **Glass:** £4.75

Car Parking: Free car park nearby

Billed as the most southerly restaurant in the British Isles, Green Island is in a hard-to-beat location right on the edge of the beach. While the terrace is perfect for summer dining, the light interior, with pale wood tables and colourful artwork is welcoming any time of year. Food is a global interpretation of local produce with an emphasis on seafood. Regular dishes like monkfish, served with stir-fried vegetables and Thai sauce, or herb-crusted brill with crab linguine, are supplemented with a range of daily specials. These may include Thai fish cakes, piquant patties of salmon and pollock; seared calves liver, juicy strips of tender meat in rich gravy with mashed potatoes; or best of all, line caught sea bass, a generous fillet of firm fish resting on wilted spinach with lemon beurre blanc. Puddings include the intriguing sounding Dom Pedro: ice cream, berries, chocolate chunks and amaretti biscuits, served like a smoothie. Service is fast and professional in the hands of the owner and a delightful waiter and waitress.

Highlight: Tasty food in a seaside-chic setting

MERCHANT HOUSE BRASSERIE

The Weighbridge, St Helier, JE2 3NF | 01534 510069
www.dolanhotels.com/merchant-house-brasserie

Opening Times: Open all day; Sandwiches 10am-6pm; Afternoon tea 3-6pm

Set Menus: Lunch two courses £12.50, three courses £15; Sunday lunch three courses £19.50

Average price two-course à la carte meal for one (excluding drinks): £22

House Wine Bottle: £15; **Glass:** £3.50 | **Car Parking:** The Esplanade

Next to Jersey Museum, the Merchant House Brasserie fulfils many functions. It is a place for afternoon tea in the sunshine, somewhere to enjoy business or pleasure lunches, to sip an excellent glass of wine after work, or to enjoy a relaxed evening meal. Thankfully, the chefs and waiters are equally adaptable. Formerly the Museum Brasserie, the restaurant has been run by Dolan Hotels since spring 2011 and shows the same emphasis on quality as Tides. The menu is a best of British, with lots of local produce like Jersey scallops, baked in a creamy sauce with mushrooms and bacon and served in the shell, or line-caught sea bass, a succulent thick fillet pan fried and accompanied by tomato chutney and herb-encrusted scampi. Puddings, which are all made in house, are British classics like custard tart, bread and butter pudding or best of all, a really moist, perfectly cooked sticky toffee pudding, served, just as it should be with vanilla ice cream and hot caramel sauce.

Highlight: Unpretentious seasonal cooking with a wide appeal for all times of the day

RESTAURANT DE LA POSTE

59 King Street, St Helier, JE2 4WE | 01534 871071 | www.delaposte.com

Opening Times: Monday-Saturday noon-2.30pm, 6-10pm
Average price two- course à la carte meal for one (excluding drinks): £24
House Wine Bottle: £15; **Glass:** £3.80 | **Car Parking:** Sand Street

In the centre of St Helier, Restaurant de la Poste overlooks King Street, Jersey's main shopping area. While its location makes it convenient for those working in town, its big windows make it a pleasant lunch spot for those at leisure too. Fake beams and an artex ceiling date the interior in the 1980s, however, the quality of the cuisine makes it feel pleasantly retro. Chef Hans creates a range of classic French dishes using fresh local produce where possible. Starters include scallops; a generous portion sizzled in bacon and garlic butter delicious mopped up with a slice of baguette; and avocado with prawns, a sumptuous green fan offset with the pale pink shellfish and a cocktail sauce. A good selection of meat mains are supplemented by catches of the day such as sea bass, two grilled fillets topped with fennel, or a slab of turbot, served with crushed Jersey Royals and a tangy caper sauce. If you have room, then puddings, such as chocolate gateaux or strawberry cheese cake, are served from a trolley.

Highlight: Generous portions of classic cuisine

FEAST

10-11 Gorey Pier, St Martin, JE3 6EW | 01534 611118 | www.feast.je

Opening Times: Tuesday-Sunday noon-2.30pm, 6-11pm
Average price two-course à la carte meal for one (excluding drinks): £20
House Wine Bottle: £14.50; **Glass:** £3.50 | **Car Parking:** Gorey Pier

Neat wooden tables and a vintage cream and red decor ensures Feast's interior befits its attractive flower-boxed frontage. While Gorey Pier is pleasant for a quick stroll, the beach and castle provide more scope for sharpening the appetite before lunch or dinner. The menu is flexible with many items available as starters or mains and served in a classic or more adventurous manner. For example, scallops can be cooked with black pudding and pancetta, or with teriyaki sauce and mango salsa; sea bass is with Jersey Royals and lemon sauce, or crab and mushroom risotto; and even the steak can be served with Béarnaise and fries or chilli garlic sauce and tiger prawns. The drinks list with its cocktails and carafes is just as user friendly with an emphasis on reasonably priced wines you can enjoy with food or quaff outside on a sunny day with a platter of nibbles.

Highlight: Jersey produce goes to Paris – quality with quirks

SAILS BRASSERIE

The Boat House, One North Quay, St Aubin
01534 744226 | www.theboathousegroup.com

Opening Times: Wednesday-Saturday 6-9.30 pm; Sunday noon-4pm

Set Menus: Sunday lunch, two courses £16.95, three courses £19.95; three-course dinner £25

House Wine Bottle: £14.95; **Glass:** £4 | **Car Parking:** Adjacent

Much more elegant than downstairs at the Boat House, Sails blurs the boundary between bistro and fine dining, ultimately defining itself as a brasserie. As you might expect for a place headed by David Cameron, a former Michelin starred chef, the menu is more extensive and refined, with items like locally farmed turbot, with ginger and scallop risotto; rack of lamb with buttered spinach; and fillet of sea bass with tomato linguini. While the view of St Aubin's harbour is definitely Jersey, and some of the produce comes from the island; the cooking travels overseas, with internationally inspired items like Thai curry or Moroccan couscous. The three-course set dinner makes Sails a good option for small groups, while the captain's table is a very pleasant semi-private space for larger groups not wishing to be totally cut off from the ambience of the restaurant.

Highlight: Being able to tell friends David Cameron cooked dinner for you

THE SALTY DOG BISTRO

Le Boulevard, St Aubin's Village,
St Brelade, JE3 8AB | 01534 742760
www.saltydogbistro.com

Opening Times: Monday-Thursday 6.30-9.30pm; Friday 12.30-2.30pm, 6.30-9.30pm; Saturday 12.30-2.30pm, 7-9.30pm; Sunday 12.30-3pm, 6.30-9.30pm

Set Menus: Three-course Sunday lunch £18.50; three-course Table d'Hôte dinner £22

Average price two-course à la carte meal for one (excluding drinks): £23

House Wine Bottle: £14; **Glass:** £3.50

Car Parking: On the road into St Aubin's wherever you can find a space

Opposite St Aubin's Harbour, The Salty Dog's summer terrace is well placed for watching boats or people while in winter, locals retreat to the cosy restaurant, where orange walls and sunny staff are an antidote to grey days. Whatever the weather, the food will lift your mood too, instantly transporting you somewhere exotic. A member of Genuine Jersey, The Salty Dog uses island grown or caught produce where possible, although the flavours veer towards Thailand, with ample use of coriander, chilli and lime. This is exemplified by dishes like sea bass, line caught, Natalie, the owner, enthuses, by one of 'our' local fishermen. Baked whole in a banana leaf with hot and sour sauce and sugar snaps, this is the ultimate fusion fish. Starters, like the pana of giant prawns, more powerful president than king, served sizzling with garlic and black bean sauce, or the Thai tuna salad, with succulent slices of seared tuna, are almost meals in themselves. Puddings such as lemony pannacotta or black butter and banana sponge, a fruity take on sticky toffee pudding, provide a finale for those with a sweet tooth.

Highlight: Fine fusion food with a great ambience

DANNY'S

The Harbour View, St Aubin's Harbour, St Brelade, JE3 8AB
01534 747306 | www.dannys.je

Opening Times: Tuesday-Thursday 5.30-9.30pm; Friday-Sunday noon-2.30pm, 5.30-9.30pm

Set Menus: Two-course lunch £16.50, three courses £19.50

Average price two-course à la carte meal for one (excluding drinks): £24

House Wine Bottle: £14.95; **Glass:** £3.95

Car Parking: Small Car Park past harbour, otherwise try for spaces near The Boat House

Exposed stone walls and chunky wooden tables set an informal tone for this St Aubin's restaurant. Chef Danny Moisan has created a lively menu which fuses Jersey produce with Asian ingredients and presents them with a New World flourish. Home baked bread with dips is a relaxed way to start a meal before moving on to items like crispy duck with a passion fruit and soy salad, tempura snapper with Thai broth, or Malay fish cakes with a zesty slaw. Main courses are named after their main ingredient – Chook is braised chicken breast with Cajun gumbo, Baargh is lamb rump with chermoula spices while Squidaroo is, quite naturally, lemon-rubbed kangaroo rumps with salt and pepper squid and tomato chutney. Cosy enough for a traditional Sunday lunch in winter, the terrace is a popular spot in summer.

Highlight: Imaginative food named to make you smile

THE GREEN OLIVE RESTAURANT

1 Anley Place, St Helier, JE2 3QE
01534 728198 | www.greenoliverestaurant.co.uk

Opening Times: Tuesday-Thursday noon-2.30pm, 6-9.30pm; Friday noon-2.30pm, 6-10pm; Saturday 6-10pm

Set Menus: Three-course early dinner £16.95

Average price two-course à la carte meal for one (excluding drinks): £21

House Wine Bottle: £13.95; **Glass:** £3.75

A dark purple door in the middle of a bright green wall is the first indication Green Olive is somewhere happy to challenge conventions. Chef/owner Paul Le Brocq was born in Jersey, trained in Jersey and buys nearly all his ingredients in Jersey, however, his flavours come from all over the world. The restaurant is also notable for not serving red meat. Instead it offers a delicious selection for vegetarians, along with plenty of choice for anyone who enjoys fish or poultry. Starters range from a simple bowl of green and black olives or a platter of hummus with toasted flat bread to pancetta grilled scallops, boldly set on a black slate in swirls of spiced sweet corn puree with refreshing apricot salsa. Main courses are equally appetising; humble chicken breasts are stuffed with peppers and feta, crispy hot samosas are crammed with sweet potato and tomato, while a confit duck leg is packed full of spices, slowly cooked and prettily presented with a pomegranate dressing.

Highlight: Fresh fusion flavours in casual town setting

INFORMAL DINING

THE QUAY BAR AND RESTAURANT

The Boat House, One North Quay, St Aubin
01534 747141 | www.theboathousegroup.com

Opening Times: Monday-Saturday noon-2.30pm, 6-9.30pm; Sunday noon-4pm
Average price two-course à la carte meal for one (excluding drinks): £14
House Wine Bottle: £14.95; **Glass:** £4 | **Car Parking:** Car park next door

Just feet away from the water, The Boat House is a stylish, glass walled structure designed to give diners and drinkers the best views of St Aubin's Harbour. The Quay Bar occupies the ground floor, with most tables located in a bright area away from the actual bar which can get a little rowdy on busy afternoons. Outside space makes The Boat House particularly popular in summer, when locals sometimes arrive by boat, mooring up just below their table. A good range of sharing platters plus simple yet substantial dishes like mussels in a cream sauce, fish pie or sausages and mash, create an easy-dining vibe. Cakes, coffees and sandwiches ensure the bar is equally suitable for lunch or a day-time snack before the music gets turned up and post-work wine drinkers arrive.

Highlight: Drinks and nibbles on the terrace

CRAB SHACK

St Brelade's Bay | 01534 744611 | www.crabshackjersey.co.uk

Opening Times: Monday 10am-2.45pm (and 5.45-8.45pm bank holidays); Tuesday-Saturday 10am-8.45pm; Sunday 10am-2.45pm, 5.45-8.45pm

Average price two-course à la carte meal for one (excluding drinks): £18

House Wine Price Bottle: £10.70; **Glass:** £2.60

Parking: Public car parks opposite

Much more than a beach-side cafe, Crab Shack caters for everything from ice-creams and sandwiches to seafood feasts. With its robust wooden tables and warm, Caribbean colour scheme, you could be anywhere in the world, until you look out of the window and take in the view of St Brelade's Bay. As with other restaurants owned by Jersey Pottery, such as the more sophisticated Oyster Box next door, there is an emphasis on fresh local produce served in large or small portions so you can decide what constitutes a starter or a main and there's also a good selection of 'shackatizers' such as breads, dips, ham or prawns to nibble. It's no surprise crabs rule the menu either, appearing as crab cakes, simply picked with salad, or whole with a mallet for you to work on yourself. Popular with families, children have their own menu and may enjoy reading you the joke panels, with delights such as 'Why did the crab cross the road?' as you sip another glass of wine.

Highlight: Family friendly quality food right off the beach

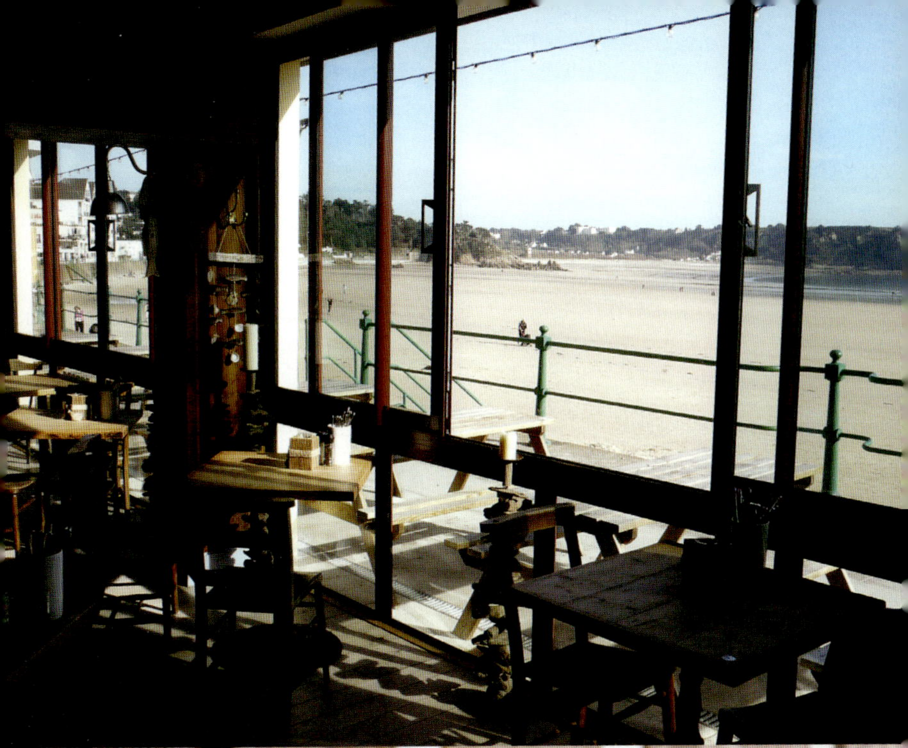

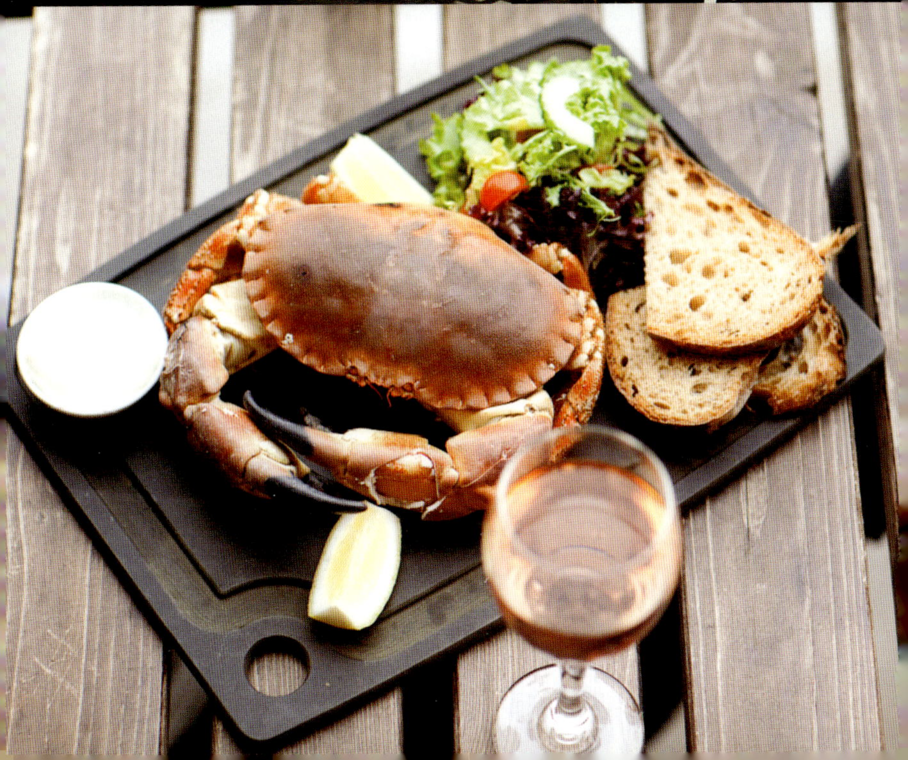

THE BEACH HOUSE

Le Mont de Ouaisne, St Brelade
01534 498 605 | www.theboathousegroup.com

Opening Times: Monday-Sunday noon-2.30pm, 6-9pm; bar open noon-9pm
Average price two-course à la carte meal for one (excluding drinks): £22
House Wine Price Bottle: £14.95; **Glass:** £3.50
Car Parking: Car park opposite restaurant

The most awkward thing about The Beach House for a non-islander is working out how to say the name of its location. Set at the bottom of Le Mont de Ouaisne (pronounced wayney), The Beach House comprises a restaurant, bar and cafe in a dark blue building overlooking the beach. At low tide you can walk here from St Brelade's but at high tide it's a short drive over the top of the headland and down the hill. The menu has an international resort feel with items like Thai curry and Mexican seared tuna, sitting alongside burgers, steaks and seafood specials. Tapas are also available for those who just fancy a snack as the waves come up. Just don't try walking back across the beach to St Brelade's if you've missed the tide.

Highlight: Alfresco dining, including BBQs

NORTH POINT BISTRO

La Rue de la Porte, Plemont, JE3 2BN | 01534 483174

Opening Times: Tuesday-Saturday 9.30am-noon breakfast, noon-2.30pm lunch, 2.30-4pm afternoon tea, 6-9pm dinner; Sunday 9.30am-noon, noon-5pm

Average price two-course à la carte meal for one (excluding drinks): £14

House Wine Price Bottle: £14.50; **Glass:** £3.95

Car Parking: On site

The North West tip of Jersey is one of the most rural parts of the island where cows outnumber people and every view is worth a photo so long as you're not blocking a tractor. Although this part of the island doesn't have many restaurants, the family-run North Point Bistro is worth the trip thanks to friendly staff and generous portions of well cooked food. Set in a pink granite building, the farm-house style interior opens onto a large courtyard ideal for family-friendly summer lunches. The menu comprises light dishes like sandwiches; including a generously filled duck wrap with crispy vegetables and hoi-sin sauce, home-made soup and Caesar salads with king prawns or Cajun chicken. For mains you find mussels in a creamy white wine sauce, home-made burgers with thick home-made chips and Italian-inspired specials. There is always a good selection of cakes, including a traditional apple pie, for anyone in for afternoon tea.

Highlight: Sun-trap courtyard lovely for a relaxed lunch

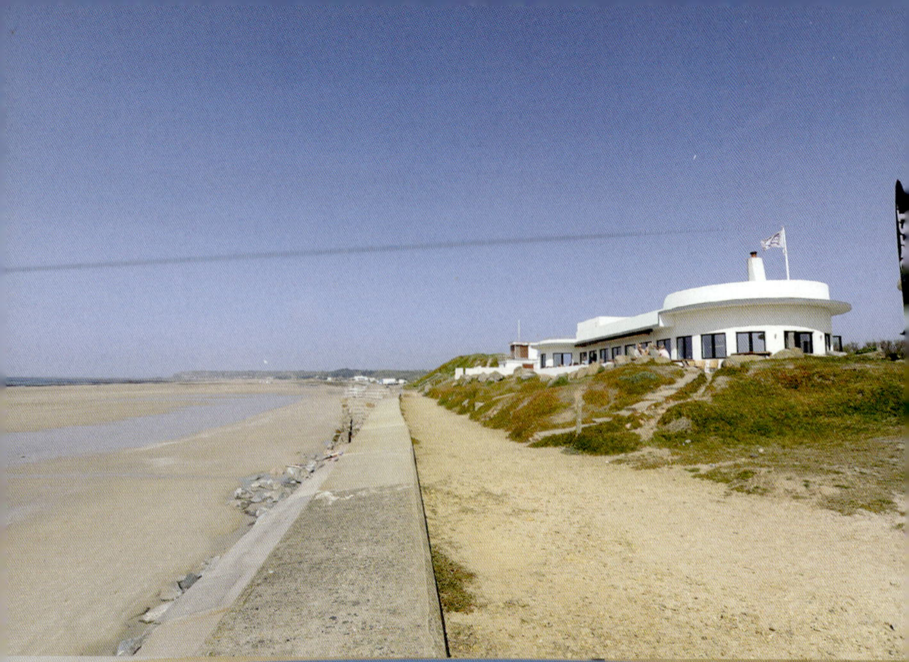

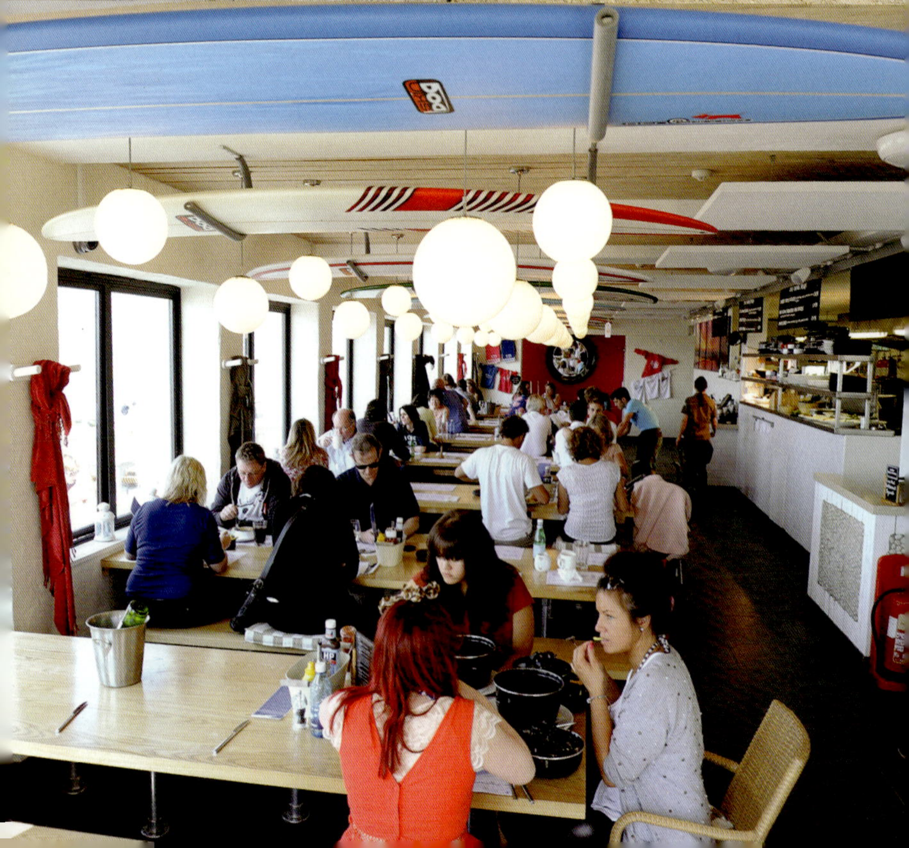

EL TICO BEACH CANTINA

St Ouen's Beach | 01534 482009 | www.elticojersey.com

Opening Times: Monday-Saturday 9am-8.30pm; Sunday 9am-7pm
Average price two-course à la carte meal for one (excluding drinks): £16
House Wine Bottle: £14.50; **Glass:** £3.95
Car Parking: On site (if it's full the restaurant will be too)

Overlooking St Ouen's Bay, El Tico's is in prime surfer territory. On a fine day you can enjoy sea views from the spacious terrace, or when it's grim sit inside by one of the large windows watching surfers brave the waves below. Bright and airy with long tables and benches, El Tico's looks like a trendy cafeteria although you do get full table service from a cheery young team in turquoise tops. Pick from a wide range of salads, platters, pizzas, pasta or spicier creations like Pad Thai, a chilli infused mound of noodles, butterflied prawns and bean sprouts. Specialities, such as mussels in a Thai broth, are chalked up on a board above the open kitchen, while beautifully iced cupcakes are temptingly set out under the counter by the entrance. All the food is freshly made with an emphasis on local suppliers. The fish and chips, a large piece of cod sealed succulently into a light crispy batter, and the Gourmet beef burger, a mammoth wedge of juicy Jersey meat served with Tallegio cheese, sun blushed tomatoes and hot slender fries, are particularly satisfying. Open all day, El Tico answers the question of where to eat outside regular hours, all be it with queues at busy times.

Highlight: Cuisine which puts the Oz into the Ouen

WAYSIDE CAFE

Le Mont Sohier, St Brelade, JE3 8BE | 01534 743915

Opening Times: Monday –Sunday 9am-8.45pm; Wednesday 9am-4.45pm
Average price two-course à la carte meal for one (excluding drinks): £15
House Wine Bottle: £11.95; **Glass:** £3.25
Car Parking: Public car parks off main road

Set above St Brelade's beach, The Wayside looks and sounds like a normal cafe. Later opening hours and substantial main courses, however, push this into somewhere you could consider for a proper meal. The terrace is a taverna-style sun trap ideal for enjoying a lazy lunch or later, for watching the sun set over the bay. As well as snacks like sandwiches, panini and salads during the day, upgrade to a tuna Niçoise and you get a cooked as requested piece of fresh fish on an appetising salad with grated carrots, Jersey Royals and black olives. Local fish, scallops and mussels also feature in a collection of mains which range from lasagna to king prawn tikka masala. The pudding cabinet is worth a look too for its decadent Jersey cream raspberry roulade, and afternoon cakes. Ice creams are also available to take back to the beach.

Highlight: Proper food served all day in informal beach-side setting

46

MURRAY'S

Norton House, St Aubin | 01534 747963
web.me.com/murraynorton1/Murrays_/Welcome.html

Opening Times: Monday-Sunday 9am-10pm

Average price two-course à la carte meal for one (excluding drinks): £15

House Wine Bottle: £14.95; **Glass:** £3.75

Car Parking: Street parking before village

From breakfast to supper with everything in-between, Murray's is one of those useful addresses where you can get a bite to eat almost any time of day, any day of the week. Owned by Murray Norton, a Jersey media presenter, the place has a personality you feel worth getting to know. A couple of leather couches make a comfy seating area for coffee, while a row of computers set against a wall of zingy flowered wall paper makes a practical internet cafe. Diners take their pick of tables, the dark wood creating a chess board effect with the paler floor. Some have a partial view of St Aubin's harbour, however; watching people walk up and down the main street is more interesting. The menu is predominantly Italian, with classic pasta dishes such as lasagne, served piping hot in a terracotta bowl, or pizzas, all of which are available in gluten-free versions. The De-Lite tastes remarkably healthy with a crispy base sprinkled with pungent goat's cheese and a mound of rocket, a guilt-free foil for a boozy glass of home-made tiramisu.

Highlight: Casual comfort food at convenient times

47

SEAFOOD

THE BASS AND LOBSTER

Gorey Coast Road, St Martin, JE3 6EU
01534 859590 | www.bassandlobster.com

Opening Times: Monday 6-9pm; Tuesday-Saturday noon-2.30pm, 6-9pm

Set Menus: Two-course lunch £10, three-course lunch £15.50 (Tuesday-Saturday) Two-course dinner £12.50, three courses £15.50 (Tuesday-Friday)

Average price two-course à la carte meal for one (excluding drinks): £25

House Wine Bottle: £15; **Glass:** £3

Thanks to its large bar and chic chocolate and vanilla decor, The Bass and Lobster flirts between being a restaurant and a gastro-pub. The chef/owner Roger White trained at Le Gavroche and opened Jersey Pottery's Oyster Box and Castle Green restaurants, a background which helps explain the classic/casual fusion. As the name suggests, local seafood is on the bill. If you are in 'restaurant' mode and go à la carte indulge in beautifully cooked seasonal specials like seared scallops with apple and black pudding, roasted lobster with tender asparagus or line-caught bass with Jersey Royals. For a more economical midweek meal, the set menu has upmarket local burgers and fish and chips alongside less ubiquitous dishes such as the crispy sweetcorn and spring onion pancake, a lightly spiced vegetable blini topped with waves of smoked salmon, or the fish and seafood assiette, substantial pieces of salmon and bass, plus prawns and mussels, served in a creamy chive sauce over wilted spinach.

Highlight: Quality food for casual dining or more indulgent meals

BISTRO ROSA

19-22 Beresford Market, St Helier, JE2 4QG | 01534 729559

Opening Times: Monday-Saturday noon-2.45pm, 6-9.30pm
Set Menus: Three courses £19.50; £23.50
Average price two-course à la carte meal for one (excluding drinks): £24
House Wine Bottle: £11.90; **Glass:** £3.60

Just inside Jersey's fish market, Bistro Rosa is an appropriate place to sample what you see on the stalls. The restaurant is casual and compact, so better suited for those who are already on close terms. Food is cooked in the open kitchen at the front so you can track the progress of your meal, although with such a small team, this can take a while at busy times. Thankfully, if you're not too ravenous to be patient, the standard of cooking means it is worth the wait. Monkfish tails are transformed into a sweet and spicy plate of coconut and lime infused medallions. Gambas sizzle with chilli oil. Scallops emerge wrapped in piping hot pancetta, while crustaceans are coaxed out of their armour to march your taste buds further than you would have imagined walking in the door. Simple sweets such as homemade pear cake or ice creams are pleasant if you have had enough pescatarian pleasures.

Highlight: Unpretentious fish dishes in bustling market bistro

50

THE OLD COURT HOUSE INN

St Aubin's Harbour, JE3 8AB | 01534 746433
www.oldcourthousejersey.com

Opening Times: Monday-Sunday 12.30-2.30pm, 7-10pm
Set Menus: Three-course Table d'Hôte £25
Average price two-course à la carte meal for one (excluding drinks): £24
House Wine Price Bottle: £14.95; **Glass:** £3.95

Set in one of Jersey's oldest buildings, The Old Court House Inn offers a range of indoor and outdoor areas to eat or drink along with rooms to stay. Overlooking St Aubin's Harbour, the 'Mizzen' restaurant in the Georgian merchants house to the front, has a nautical theme with wooden walls and blue upholstery, while the front terrace is a lively spot. Further back, in a part of the building dating back to 1450, the 'Judges Chamber' is a traditional haven with stone walls and polished oak, or for fine days, the 'Courtyard Restaurant' is a brighter option. The menu has a range of seafood, including a sharing platter, along with lobster, crab, oysters and mussels. For starters, the prawn cocktail is a classic juxtaposition of large prawns, lettuce and creamy Marie-Rose. Soup changes daily, however, carrot and courgette, served with hunks of fresh crusty baguette, tastes aptly of its ingredients. Mains are predominantly fish and include grilled Jersey plaice, halibut with asparagus and dill, salmon with scallops and pea puree and a fish dish of the day. Meat options are more limited with a choice of steaks or lamb while a separate bistro menu is also available in bar areas.

Highlight:
Atmospheric historic setting open every day

THE OYSTER BOX

The Oyster Box, St Brelade's Bay, Jersey, JE3 8EF
01534 743311 | www.oysterbox.co.uk

Opening Times: Monday 6-9.30pm; Tuesday–Thursday noon-2.30pm, 6-9.30pm; Friday - Saturday noon-2.30pm, 6-10pm; Sunday noon-3pm, 6-9.30pm

Average price two-course à la carte meal for one (excluding drinks): £28

House Wine Bottle: £15; **Glass:** £3.80

Car Parking: Opposite

Poached, grilled or simply chilled, however you like your Royal Bay Noisettes or Special No. 3s, Oyster Box has it covered. As well as locally cultivated molluscs, the restaurant, which is run by Jersey Pottery, serves a spectrum of fresh seafood, sustainable fish and quality meat. Overlooking St Brelade's Bay, the best time to visit is early on a summer evening. As sun descends into the waves, a team of young waitresses bustle around tables, making sure your glass is never long at low tide. Dishes are casually chic like the decor and the diners, and many are available as large or small portions to suit your appetite. Scallops are usually a good call, lightly sautéed with lobster ravioli and wilted spinach as are tempura prawns, large presents of crisp batter begging to be crunched open and dipped into a chilli sauce. For mains, a roast fillet of turbot, with an innovative lobster and lime gnocchi or pan-fried brill with Jersey Royals are tasty takes on local produce.

Highlight: Consistently good food and ambience

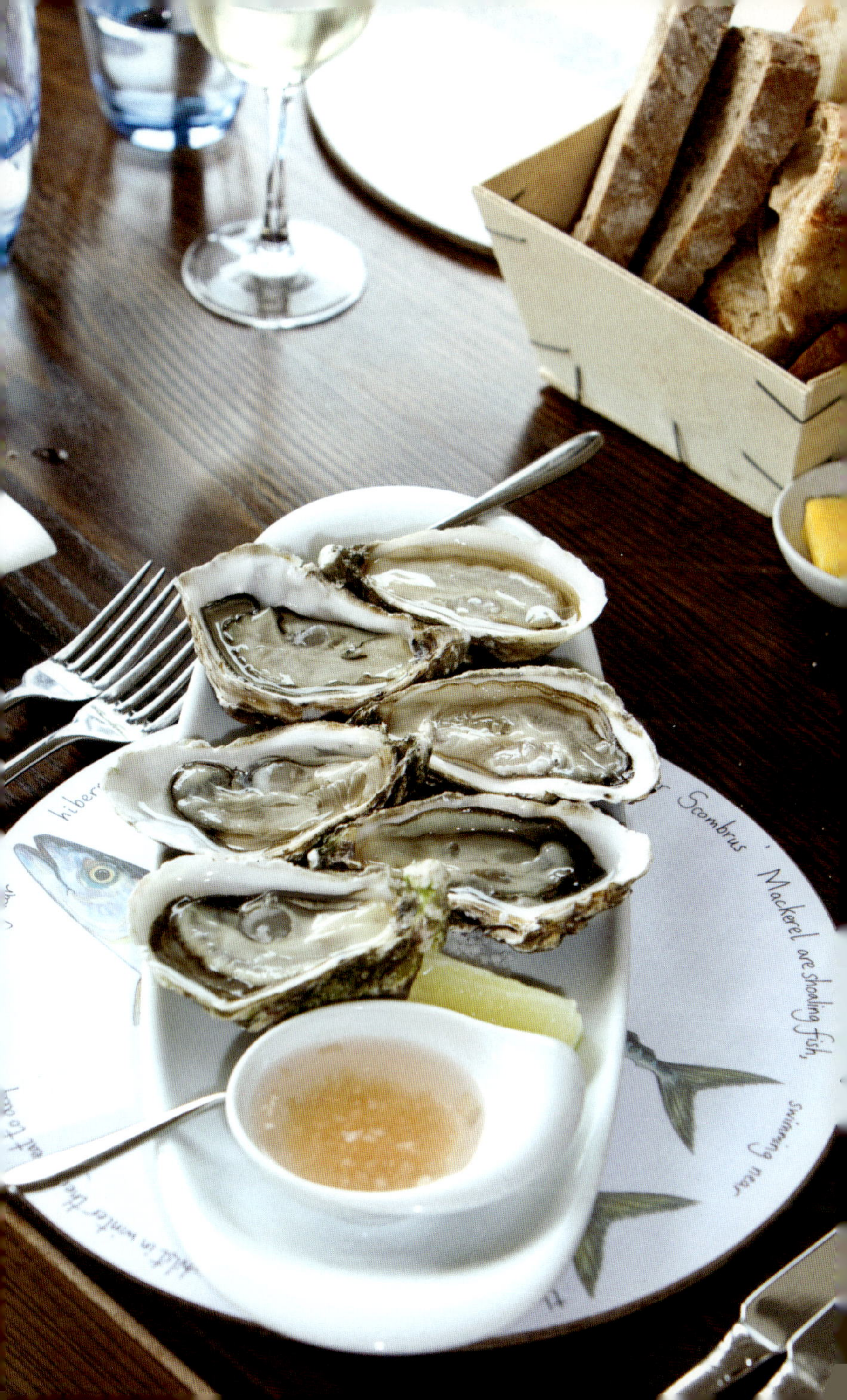
Scombrus
Mackerel are shoaling fish,
swimming near

ROSEVILLE BISTRO

86 Roseville Street | 01534 874259 | www.rosevillebistro.com

Opening Times: Tuesday-Sunday 5.30-10pm (closed January)
Set Menus: Two-course early dinner £13.50, three courses £16.50
Average price two-course à la carte meal for one (excluding drinks): £24
House Wine Bottle: £14.95; **Glass:** £4.25
Parking: On street places very limited. Green Street a fair walk.

Tucked away on a residential street near Havre de Pas lido, The Roseville Bistro began business more than 40 years ago and is now owned by the founder's daughter. Decorated with maritime memorabilia, the intimate original room leads to a more spacious conservatory with exposed stone walls. While crab and prawn sandwiches made up early menus, they have expanded into a solid selection of fish and seafood plus char-grilled steaks, although shellfish still reins. Choose from starters like local scallops, baked in an earthenware dish with a creamy bacon and spring onion sauce, or crab cakes, two crispy portions of white crab meat, pepped up with chilli sauce and a delicious salad, or, best of all, the crab cocktail, a glass of freshly picked crab on avocado and lettuce, so sweet and soft it can be eaten like ice-cream. Mains are uncomplicated dishes designed to show off the fish with whatever flavours please the customer. However, again, shellfish is still a forerunner, with dishes like half lobster, simply grilled with garlic butter, oodles of king prawns, perfect fries and a delicious salad, triumphing.

Highlight: Superb shellfish

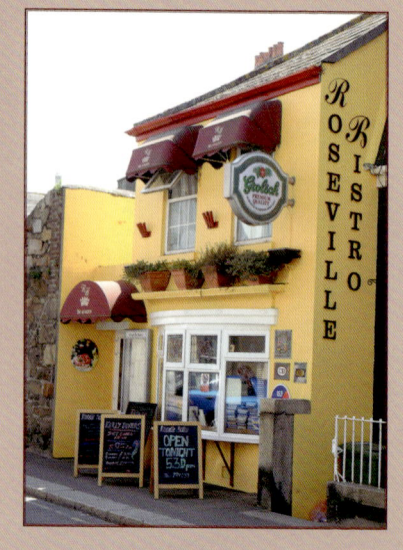

ATLANTIQUE SEAFOOD BAR

8-10 West Centre, Bath Street, St Helier, JE2 4ST
01534 720052 | www.atlantiqueseafood.com

Opening Times: Monday-Saturday 9am-11pm all day service

Average price two-course à la carte meal for one (excluding drinks): £25

House Wine Bottle: £16; **Glass:** £3.75

With saffron walls and large white lanterns, you might initially mistake the Atlantique for an oriental restaurant; however, once you clock lobster pots at the back and open the menu all is clear. For seafood purists there are platters of local produce such as crab, mussels and Royal Bay oysters served naturally or with more adventurous flavours like wasabi or Bloody Mary. For those who prefer fish there is a wide selection of items like whole roasted Jersey bass, served with a side plate of potatoes and curried vegetables, or a daily special, such as a surprisingly succulent fillet of hake, wrapped in bacon and topped with langoustines. Starters are mostly fish based too, like a king prawn and squid tempura, with mango sauce and toasted nut and sweet pepper salad. The large round table in the window is a lovely spot for a group, while the spacious terrace, next to the bronze cows, is one of St Helier's best alfresco options. Tapas are available from 3-6pm, perfect for those who prefer marinated octopus to cupcakes.

Highlight: All day dining with a strong emphasis on local seafood

MEDITERRANEAN

LA CANTINA

7 Pierson Road, Westpark, St Helier, JE2 3PD
01534 724988 | www.lacantinajersey.com

Opening Times: Monday 6-10.30pm; Tuesday-Saturday noon-2.00pm, 6-10.30pm

Average price two-course à la carte meal for one (excluding drinks): £18

House Wine Bottle: £13; **Glass:** £3.50

Car Parking: Patriotic Street (most on-street spaces nearby are resident only)

While many restaurants source ingredients from a market, La Cantina's chefs are just as likely to forage Jersey hedgerows for choice fare. Nettle gnocchi and scallops with wild garlic are a couple of creative specials inspired by whatever is in season. The restaurant makes its own fresh pasta every day, the first of its kind accredited by Genuine Jersey, and uses a wide range of local produce in all of its dishes along with Italian olive oils, wines and other delicacies. Flavours are rustic Italian, using traditional recipes handed down to La Cantina owner Marcus Calvani and even the simplest dishes are elevated with quality ingredients. Pastas include pappardelle al sugo di lepre, thick ribbons of fresh pasta with a sauce of Tuscan wild hare, asparagus and mascarpone, while pizzas are baked in a stone-oven, and served with toppings such as grilled aubergines, fresh tomato and Genuine Jersey Luganega sausage. Puddings, like the affogato; icecream and espresso with crushed Cantucci biscuits and a shot of Amaretto, are equally enticing.

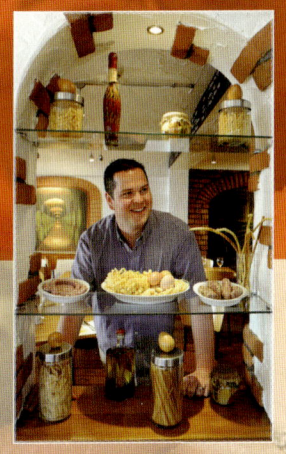

Highlight: Fresh enthusiastic cooking which transcends its genre

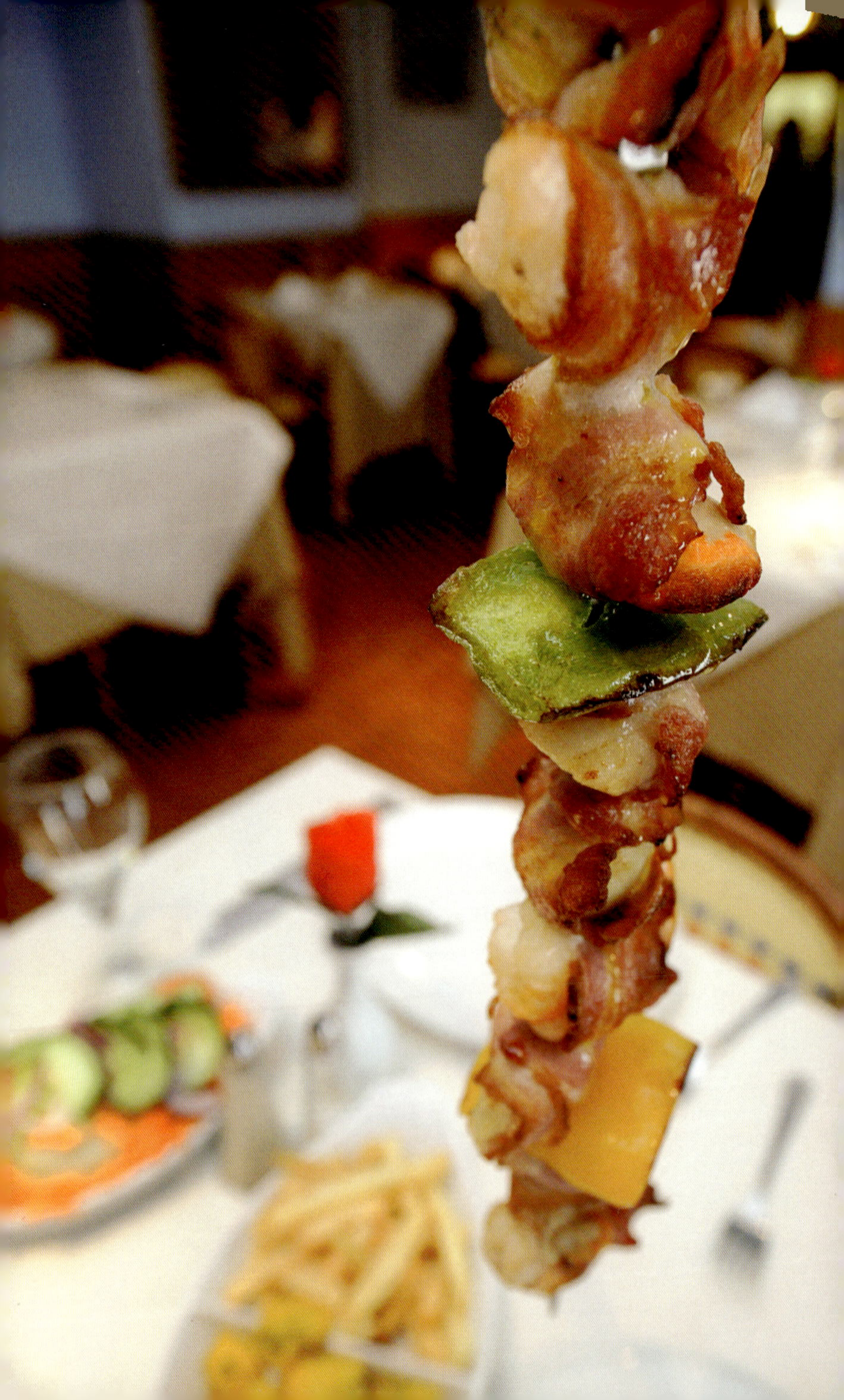

RESTAURANT DO PORTO

3 Minden Street, St Helier | 01534 632969

Opening Times: Monday-Sunday noon-2.30pm; 6-10.30pm
Average price two-course à la carte meal for one (excluding drinks): £17
House Wine Price Bottle: £11.25; **Glass:** £3 | **Car Parking:** Minden Place

Its name evokes images of a bustling harbour, fishing boats bobbing in the water and sardine smoke in the air. The actual setting for Restaurant Do Porto is less romantic as it's above a Portuguese grocery store opposite a multi-storey car park. Nevertheless, if you are looking for delicious Portuguese food in Jersey, this is one of the most authentic places to come. The house speciality is espedatas, long kebabs of grilled meat or fish, served from hooks at the table. Options include the Terra and Mar, a surf and turf combo with beef and jumbo pieces of succulent shellfish; 'Tradicional' involves several hundred grams of rare, garlic marinated steak; while chicken, offers generous chunks of moist, perfectly cooked chicken breast. These are all accompanied by salad, savoury rice and crispy cubes of fried herb polenta. The clientele include plenty of Portuguese, with weekend nights often full of families, couples and the occasional large group, and while the restaurant is quiet during the day, come evening it can get pretty lively.

Highlight: Fabulous espedatas for a good value meal

GIO'S RESTAURANT

58 Halkett Place, St Helier | 01534 736733 | www.giosrestaurant.com

Opening Times: Monday-Saturday noon-1.45pm; 6.30-9.30pm

Set Menus: Three-course lunch £15

Average price two-course à la carte meal for one (excluding drinks): £20

House Wine Bottle: £17.40; **Glass:** £2.90

Car Parking: Minden Place

With its red and white checked table cloths and ever-present owner, Gio's is a taste of Italy, and in particular, of Venice, in the centre of town. As with many traditional restaurants, you can opt for the menu or the board, which has a choice selection of specials such as asparagus, carpaccio, Dover sole or calves' liver, two long slices of meat, cooked in a light batter with red wine and sage. À la carte the extensive menu offers both pasta and other Italian dishes like escalope Milanese, a flattened, bread crumbed piece of veal, along with classic international options like smoked salmon, beef stroganoff or duck in orange sauce. Most items are served by themselves so separate orders of salad or vegetables are required. For afters, choose from fruit with zabaione, cassata, tiramisu, and ice cream, or just feast your eyes on one of the colourful boxes of panettone, perched above the room on dark wooden beams.

Highlight: Classical Italian cuisine ideal for city lunches

LITTLE ITALY

36 Kensington Place, St Helier | 01534 720631 | www.littleitalyjersey.com

Opening Times: Tuesday-Sunday 6-10pm
Average price two-course à la carte meal for one (excluding drinks): £18
House Wine Bottle: £11.50; **Glass:** £2.90 | **Car Parking:** Patriotic Street

With its open kitchen and genuine Italian staff, Little Italy has a lively, trattoria ambience perfect for a casual supper. Whether it is due to location, price or simply the ambience, this restaurant always seems busy. The menu includes everything you would expect for an Italian restaurant outside Italy with pastas, pizzas, hot and cold starters and traditional main courses like chicken wrapped in Parma ham, pork with mushrooms, or grilled fish. While the pizzas, hand-made at the counter, are much smaller than in American-style pizzerias, pasta dishes are copious. A lasagne comes with more cheese than X-Factor, while Penne Siciliana, a mammoth portion of aubergines, chilli, tomato and melted mozzarella, continues steaming long past the point where your appetite might be satiated. Popular with everyone from hen parties to romantic couples, the waiters and waitresses buzz about like Vespas in a piazza.

Highlight: Lively trattoria where food is served hotter than Etna

LA CAPANNINA

65-67 Halkett Place, St Helier | 01534 734602

Opening Times: Monday–Saturday noon-2pm, 7-10pm
Average price two-course à la carte meal for one (excluding drinks): £35
House Wine Bottle: £22; **Glass:** £7 | **Car Parking:** Minden Place

One of the last places in Jersey to offer full silver service, La Capannina is the sort of restaurant that has been doing things the same way for over 30 years. The pine clad walls provide a warm backdrop for well spaced tables elegantly set with white linen, engraved glasses and silver cutlery. Meals usually commence with small squares of warm cheese and tomato pizza as the first in a fleet of Italian waiters dressed in black-tie take your order. Fine wines proliferate the list for anyone wanting to spoil themselves, while the menu is supplemented by a selection of specials such as roast saddle of lamb or sea bass with fennel. Dishes like grilled asparagus, propped at the perfect angle to maximise butter distribution, or crab salad, a mound of white meat offset with a twist of green, are freshly uncomplicated. Main courses include escalope Milanese, a vast spread of bread-crumbed veal, and sole, cooked with butter and lemon, deftly de-boned near the table, showing off the waiter's skills as much as the kitchen's. The pudding trolley trundles out scrumptious classics; bowls of raspberries, a collection of pannacotta and the ubiquitous creamy coffee combo of tiramisu.

Highlight: Fabulous service in a classic cocoon

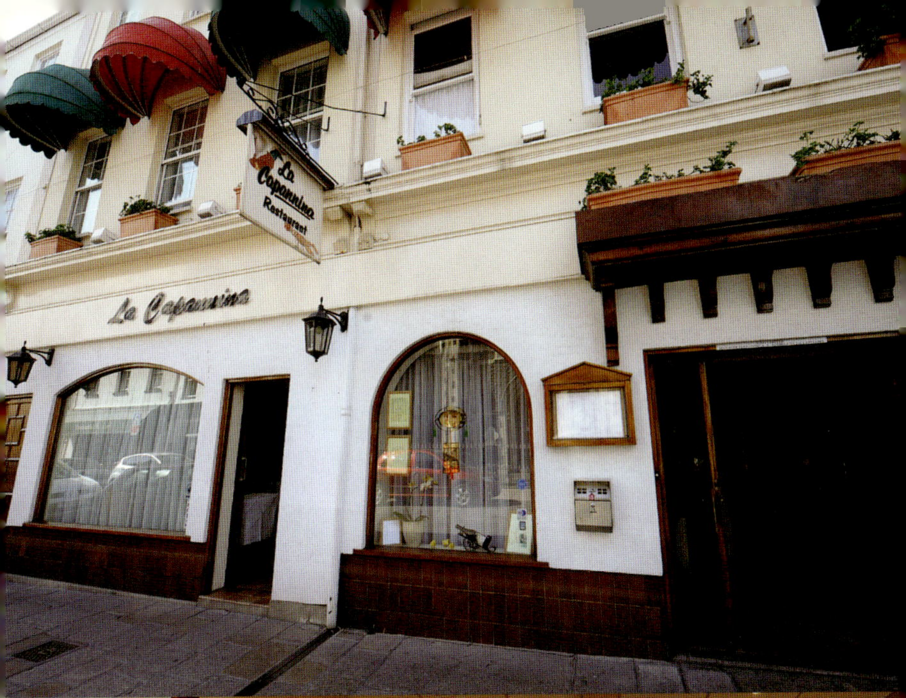
La Capannina
Restaurant
La Capannina

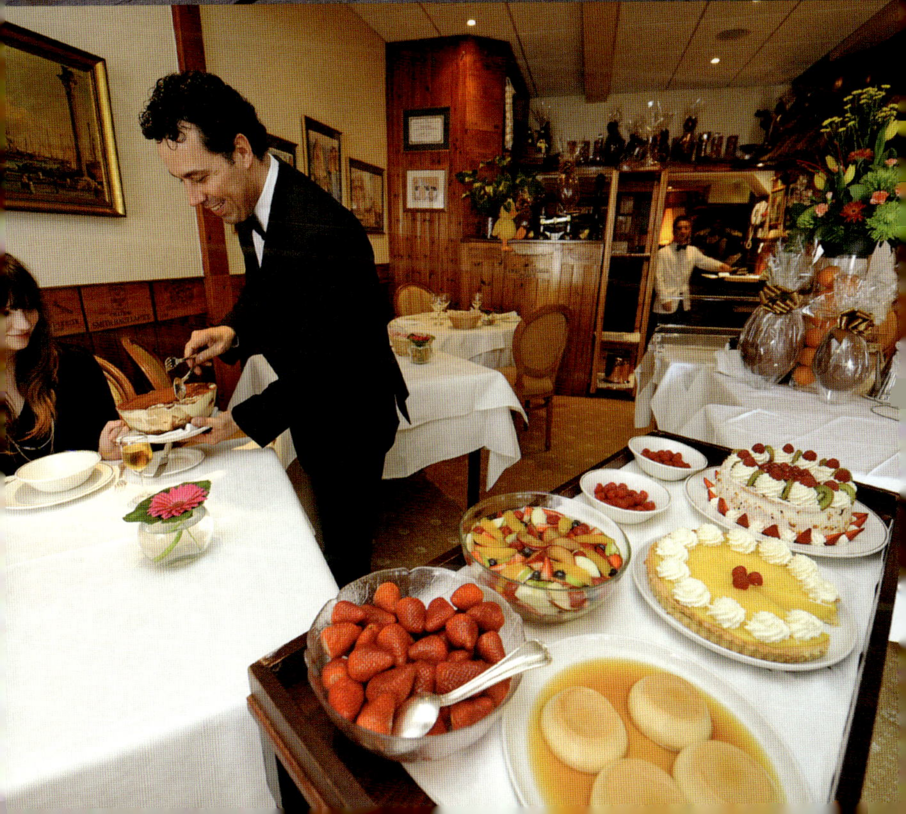

ASIAN

BONNE NUIT BEACH CAFE

La Charrières de Bonne Nuit, St John, JE3 4DD
01534 861656 | www.bonnenuitbeachcafe.com

Opening Times: Monday-Sunday 9am-5pm;
Thai evenings Thursday-Sunday 5.30-8.45pm (March-November)

Average price two-course à la carte meal for one (excluding drinks): £12

House Wine: BYOB

Car Parking: Outside if you're lucky or on the left hand side going back up the hill

You're not dreaming if you think you can smell Thai food coming from Bonne Nuit Bay. Just as the beach is totally transformed between low tide and high tide, the cafe also has two completely different sides. If you fancy a bacon roll and a mug of coffee, sandwiches, jacket potatoes or afternoon tea with scones, you will be amply catered for. However, should you feel like something more exotic in the evening, there's a wide range of Thai options to choose, just remember to bring your own wine or beer. There are only two woks so food for groups can arrive at different times making it wise to order a few nibbles first if you are famished. Dishes include Thai favourites such as green curry, made as mild or hot as you like with a choice of meat; sizzling stir fries and Pad Thai, a mass of spicy king prawns nestling in oodles of steaming noodles. While views of the beach distract your eye during the day, the casual decor is less atmospheric at night, although there's a full take away menu so you can also enjoy the food in the comfort of your own home.

Highlight: An unexpected taste of Thailand on Jersey's north coast

BENTO

1 Commercial Street, St Helier, JE2 3RU
01534 887577 | www.bentosushi.co.uk

Opening Times: Monday-Friday 11.30am-10pm; Saturday noon-10pm (last orders 9.30pm)

Average price two-course à la carte meal for one (excluding drinks): £15

House Wine Bottle: £13; **Glass:** £3.50

Car parking: The Esplanade

With their respective red and white flags and love of fresh seafood, Jersey and Japan have more in common than you might imagine, especially on one street corner in St Helier. Bento combines Jersey produce with Japanese ideas to create food which is fast, fresh and even fun. Multi-colour plates priced from £1.60-£5, whizz around a central conveyor belt like culinary trains on a track. Ingredients include local eggs, crabs, scallops, sea bass and island-grown shitake mushrooms, alongside sustainable Scottish salmon and non-endangered Yellow fin Tuna. After nibbling a few plates of sushi, or Endamame beans, the kitchen produces excellent hot dishes such as Kaisen Udon, thick wheat noodles coiled around chilli-seared scallops, spring onions and mint; Katsu Curry, patties of butternut squash; or Tempura prawns, giant prawns in a crisp, light batter. Beer drinkers get a choice of Japanese brews, while if you prefer to nosh at your desk or go somewhere pretty for a picnic, take-away Bento boxes are available.

Highlight: Say sayonara to sushi once you smell the hot dishes.

JAIPUR

20 Esplanade, St Helier, JE2 3QA | 01534 880069 | www.jaipur-jersey.co.uk

Opening Times: Open every day noon-2pm; 6pm-midnight

Set Menus: Two courses £14.95

Average price two-course à la carte meal for one (excluding drinks): £16

House Wine Bottle: £12.95; **Glass:** £3.75

Car Parking: The Esplanade

Named after India's pink city, Jaipur's brilliant white frontage and magenta lights are a temple to contemporary Indian cuisine. Attentive waiters bustle between tables, quickly seating newcomers before sorting out delicious smelling bags of food for those who prefer to drop by and take meals home. The menu covers everything you would expect from Indian cuisine, with a good selection of popular dishes like chicken tikka masala, a bowl of bright red, lightly spiced meat; and more unusual offerings such as lamb manipur, a mild and sweet Keralan curry with chunks of mango and banana, or Nali Nihari slow cooked lamb shank. Opposite the bus station, Jaipur is popular both with couples sharing a relaxed meal and larger groups celebrating an event.

Highlight: Good Indian food in a contemporary setting

GRILLS

THE GRILL

The Royal Yacht, Weighbridge, St Helier, JE2 3NF
01534 720511 | www.theroyalyacht.com

Opening Times: Monday-Sunday 11am-11pm (last food orders 10pm)
Average price two-course à la carte meal for one (excluding drinks): £22
House Wine Bottle: £17; **Glass:** £4 | **Car Parking:** The Esplanade

Before The Royal Yacht turned into a slick super-cruiser, the hotel could have been likened to a classic schooner where you could hide from the elements with a stiff drink. The Grill, at the inner core of the hotel, is still like this. White washed brick walls, a long wooden bar and dark blue high chairs create a timeless setting where you could just as easily imagine a ship's captain in full uniform sitting down next to you as a hedge fund boss. The nature of the room with its bar seating means it works well if you are eating by yourself or with one other person; however, there are also a few tables for small groups. Aimed firmly at carnivores, the menu is all about meat and in particular, steaks. Whether you like T-Bone, fillets, sirloin, rump or even chateaubriand, it should be one of the tenderest, juicy pieces of meat you will eat on the island. Steak dishes include crispy chips and grilled vine tomatoes, mushrooms and a choice of sauce.

Highlight: Classic comfort food ideal for solo or duet dining

CANDLELIGHT RESTAURANT

The Revere Hotel, Kensington Place, St Helier, JE2 3PA
01534 611111 | www.jerseyrooms.co.uk

Opening Times: Monday-Sunday 6-9.45pm (Friday and Saturdays only in January/February)

Average price two-course à la carte meal for one (excluding drinks): £25

House Wine Price Bottle: £15.50; **Glass:** £3.20

Car Parking: Patriotic Street

With its ancient castle style decor and fabulous wine list The Candlelight is not your typical grill, however, with a menu dominated by meat, it is natural to head in this direction. Steaks include fillet or sirloin, served with traditional accompaniments like chunky chips, pepper sauce and grilled tomatoes although specialities such as the Chateaubriand or Drunken Bullock, a sabre-impaled sirloin, are served flamboyantly at your table for just a little more. The cooking is predominantly French, with mains like rack of lamb, three pieces of tender pink meat perched in a Bordeaux-style bean cassoulet.

Prices are reasonable for the quality of produce with beautifully presented dishes and elevating touches such as home-made bread. Market specials such as a starter of asparagus, goat's cheese and Parma ham, deliciously offset with a fresh mango and tomato salsa, as well as scrummy puddings, show the chef's talents extend far beyond meat.

Highlight: French cooking and fine wines in a romantic setting

WILDFIRE

14 Mulcaster Street, St Helier, JE2 3NJ
01534 625555 | www.wildfirejersey.com

Opening Times: Monday-Sunday upstairs Grill from noon-2.30pm and 6pm-10pm; Tapas downstairs from 10am-10pm

Set Menus: two-course lunch or pre-theatre menu £15; three course set lunch or dinner for groups of 10 or more £25

Average price two-course à la carte meal for one (excluding drinks): £25

House Wine Bottle: £12.95; **Glass:** £3.25 | **Car Parking:** Sand Street

Divided into two zones, Wildfire comprises a first floor grill and cocktail bar and a downstairs tapas restaurant and lounge bar both stylishly decorated in black and white. A carnivore's paradise, Wildfire has one of the island's biggest selections of steaks from freshly cut rib eyes to 21-day aged Aberdeen Angus fillets. Items like the Chateaubriand, (£35 for two to share), a sumptuous piece of coal-grilled meat, are served on a wooden board with grilled tomatoes and deep-fried onion twists, accompanied by a choice of sauce. Vegetables, such as buttered green beans, or crispy hand-cut chips, are extra. The set menus and central location make the restaurant popular with groups of friends or colleagues, although metallic curtains and deep booths with cow-hide seats give couples more privacy.

Highlight: Tender steaks cooked just as requested

PUB DINING

St MARY'S Country

LA RUE DE
LA VALLÉE

ST MARY'S COUNTRY INN

La Rue des Buttes, St Mary, JE3 3DS
01534 482897 | www.liberationgroup.com

Opening Times: Monday-Sunday noon-2.30pm; 6-9pm

Average price two-course à la carte meal for one (excluding drinks): £16

House Wine Bottle: £12.50; **Glass:** £3.10

Billed as a placed for 'relaxed drinking and dining', St Mary's Country Inn walks a tipsy line between being a pub and a restaurant. Tables close to the bar, which serves locally brewed Liberation Ales and Mary Ann beers, are more atmospheric, yet those in the bold wallpapered dining room are more comfortable for a substantial meal, an easy choice when you consider the generous portions. The menu is divided into nine sections; from interesting nibbles like chilli olives and feta, through starters such as homemade soup, halves like a warm Jersey Blue cheese and pear salad, to roasts, espedatas and mains. Here you find more 'restauranty' options like pan-fried fillet of sea bass served with new potatoes and tomato haricots, tucked alongside pub-grub classics like scampi, burgers and southern fried chicken. The menu continues with platters, sides and finally huge, wicked looking desserts which feature Willy Wonka Factory quantities of chocolate, cream and other diet-busting delights. More gusto than gastro, cooking is still competent enough to fill most hungry tummies.

Highlight: One of the prettiest pubs in Jersey

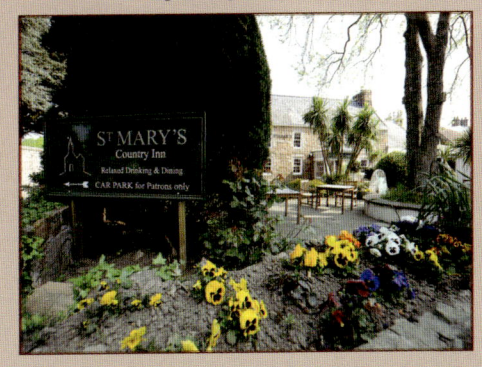

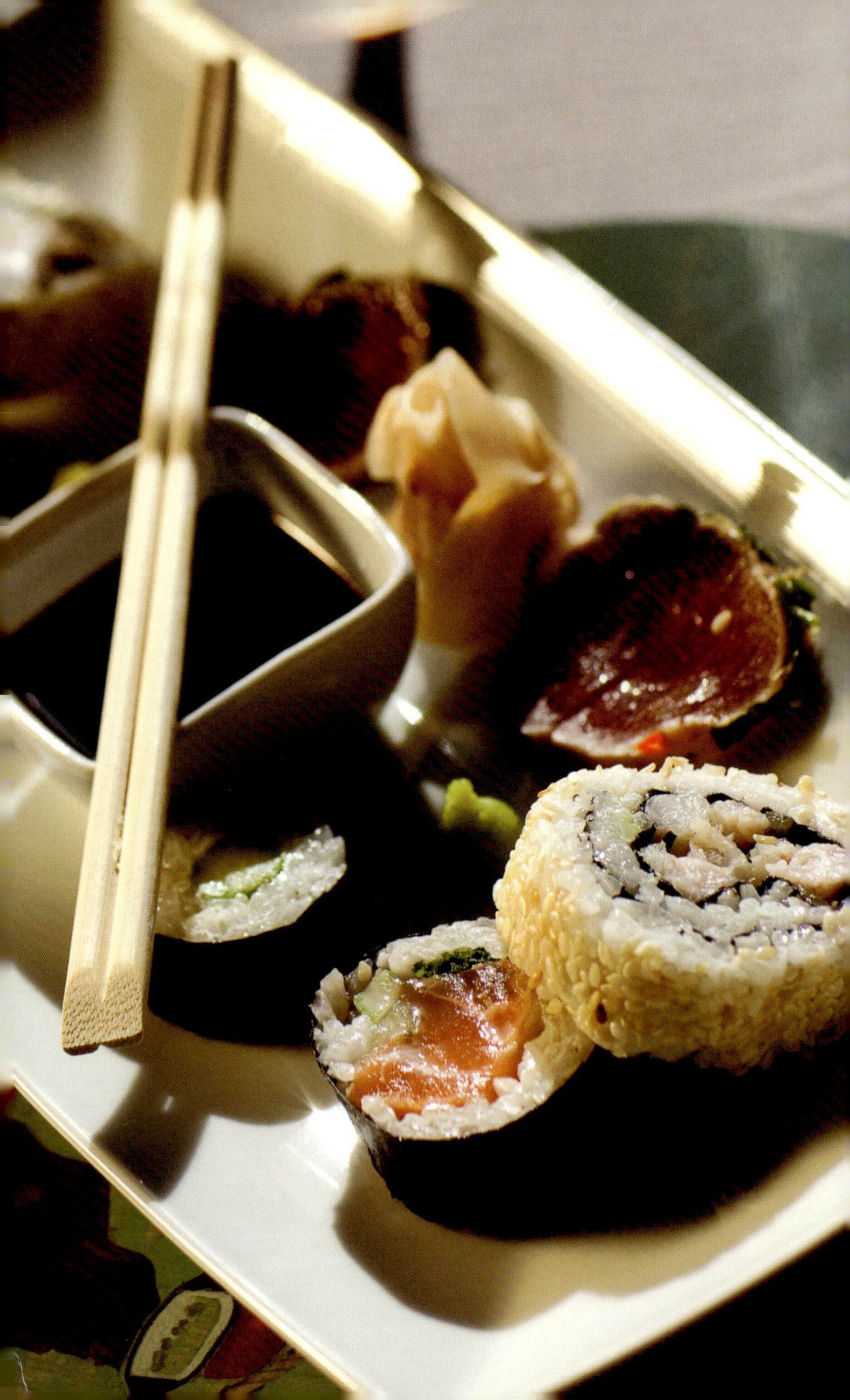

CASTLE GREEN GASTROPUB

La Route de la Cote, St Martin, JE3 6DR
01534 840218 | www.castlegreenjersey.co.uk

Opening Times: Tuesday-Thursday noon-2.30pm, 6-8.30pm; Friday-Saturday noon-2.30pm, 6.30-9pm; Sunday 10.30am-3pm

Average price two-course à la carte meal for one (excluding drinks): £23

House Wine Bottle: £14; **Glass:** £3.35

Although billed as a gastro-pub, despite the presence of a bar it would be difficult to wander into Castle Green and only order a drink. A champion of Genuine Jersey, the menu is covered with stamps signifying ingredients are island grown or caught. Owned by Jersey Pottery, the 'pub' has effectively become the Oyster Box of the east thanks to its informal atmosphere, sea views and excellent food. While some dishes change during the year to reflect what is in season, there is a strong Mediterranean influence, especially with starters which are designed to work as individual portions or platters to share. Items of note include the antipasto, with full flavoured Parma ham, roasted vegetables and leaves drizzled with fruity olive oil, and the scallops, seared and served with a creamy, rich, butternut squash risotto. Classics such as the rib-eye steak, a generous piece of tender meat, served with super-hot chips ensure the venue is as appealing for a cosy winter lunch as for a sunny, summer dinner.

Highlight: Excellent use of local and international ingredients for a real gastro-pub experience

LE HOCQ INN

La Grande Route de la Cote, St Clement, JE2 6PF | 01534 854924

Opening Times: Monday-Saturday noon-2pm, 6-9pm (earlier closing in winter); Sunday noon-2pm, 6-8pm

Average price two-course à la carte meal for one (excluding drinks): £17

House Wine Bottle: £14.50; **Glass:** £3.55

Car Parking: Large car park next to Parish Hall

While seagulls can be a nuisance if they get too close to your lunch, the sight of birds swooping over wave-washed rocks a few hundred yards from your table is quite mesmerising. The occasional car passing along the coast road ensures there's no chance of being hypnotised by the view, although after a full meal at Le Hocq you might need a snooze to digest. Painted cream, just like the exterior, Le Hocq's restaurant is a bright space, simply furnished with coir matting, pine tables and photos of the local coastline. The chef uses mostly local produce to create a pleasing menu of pub classics like fish and chips or home-made burgers, along with more elegant offerings such as baked bream, perched on a round of crushed Jersey Royals with asparagus and Hollandaise. And, although that sounds lovely, you're likely to get food envy once you smell the roast beef, served with Yorkshire puddings, gravy and a bowl of fresh vegetables. Puddings are home-made with options like treacle sponge, a large moist square of syrup-drenched sponge, and custard, offering a hearty end to a meal. The more calorie-conscious could finish with a drink on the terrace or in the cosy bar next door with the gorgeous resident Labrador.

Highlight: Easy-going food for summer or winter with a sea view

LE MOULIN DE LECQ

Le Mont de la Greve de Lecq, St Ouen, JE3 2DT
01534 482818 | www.moulindelecq.com

Opening Times: Monday-Saturday noon-2pm, 6-9pm;
Sunday noon-3pm, 6-9pm

Average price two-course à la carte meal for one (excluding drinks): £17

House Wine Bottle: £11.90; **Glass:** £3.20

With its leafy garden and inviting granite frontage, The Moulin de Lecq looks like a country pub, yet this 600 year old former watermill is just a few yards away from one of the island's most popular beaches. From Easter to September blue Tantivy buses disgorge streams of day trippers onto this small sandy cove, however, it is much calmer in the evenings should you fancy a quiet drink in the traditional beamed bar or a casual bite to eat in the light pine restaurant. The menu has a Mediterranean vibe, using Jersey grown vegetables and local fish for dishes like whole baked mackerel, served with a tangy caper sauce, crisp batons of carrots and new potatoes. Meat-lovers are also well catered for with cooked as requested fillet steak and chips, the most expensive item on the menu, costing less than £16. Puddings, like chocolate fudge cake, actually a slab of wonderfully gooey chocolate and caramel tart, are impressively home made.

Highlight: Good value food in family-friendly environment

CAFES

PLEMONT BEACH CAFE

Plemont, St Ouen | 01534 482005

Opening Times: Monday-Sunday 9am-5pm (breakfast served until 11.30am weekdays, 11.45am weekends). July/August open until 6pm; June-September Fridays until 8pm

Average price two-course à la carte meal for one (excluding drinks): £13

House Wine Bottle: £10; **Glass:** £3.65

Car Parking: Limited spaces outside, more in car park at top of hill

Jersey's massive tidal range is displayed to stunning effect at Plemont. At high tide turquoise waves wash over the entire beach, while just a few hours later, the sea retreats to reveal a golden sandy cove dimpled with pools and caves. Of course, the colour scheme is quite different on a grey day when you will be glad to sit inside the cream and blue room, decorated with local art work and ceramics, trying to spot puffins nesting on the cliffs, or just contemplating the scenery. Genuine Jersey produce dominates a menu which covers all appetites from full cooked breakfasts to light afternoon teas. Freshly made soup, paninis and sandwiches are available for lunches, along with home-made Jersey beef burgers, steak and chips and salads. Cakes, such as the carrot cake, a substantial slice of dark sticky sponge flecked with carrots and raisins, are rather good and are all made with local eggs. Particularly popular with locals for breakfast, there is a good sized terrace for sunny days, well placed to maximise the view.

Highlight: Breakfast in the sunshine after a walk on the beach

THE GUNSITE CAFE

La Route de la Haule, St Peter, JE3 7YD | 01534 735806

Opening Times: Monday-Sunday 8am-5pm

Average price two-course à la carte meal for one (excluding drinks): £8

Car Parking: A handful of scratch card spaces outside (one unit for two hours)

Set in a former gun turret built by the Germans during World War II, The Gunsite Cafe is in a convenient position mid-way between St Helier and St Aubin's so don't be confused the address is St Peter's. Thick concrete walls, whitewashed from within, make the cafe a cool retreat from the sun although the cafe is just as useful a shelter for warming up on winter beach walks. Cooked breakfasts are a speciality, while a counter full of yummy looking cakes is likely to tempt those just stopping for a coffee. There is a good selection for a light lunch with items like baked potatoes, filled with a piquant tuna mayonnaise, sandwiches and wraps, such as the chicken breast and red peppers, dressed with sweet chilli sauce, offering healthier alternatives. Picnic benches provide seating overlooking the beach in a prime position for watching the hobie cats and sand yachts, while sporty customers can forget their cars as the cafe is next to the cycle track.

Highlight: Casual cafe convenient for cycle-track snacks.

COLLEEN'S CAFE

Greve de Lecq, St Ouen, JE3 2DL | 01534 481420

Opening Times: Monday-Sunday 8.30am-5pm

Average price two-course à la carte meal for one (excluding drinks): £10

House Wine Bottle: £11.95; **Glass** £3.95

Car Park: Limited availability outside cafe, however plentiful parking near entrance to beach

A true beach cafe, fish and chips, sandwiches and full cooked breakfasts are all staples at Colleens. While the inside is fresh and neutral with ample seating for winter customers; on sunny days most people end up relaxing on the terrace or taking one of the tables for two on the veranda. Cakes, made on the premises by the owner, Adam Queree, are some of the most scrumptious on the island. The orange drizzle cake, a sumptuous sponge full of almonds, citrus zest and coconut, is the sort of bikini-busting bake which inspires a hike along the cliff paths, rather than a session on the sun lounger. Just a few metres back from the beach, towards the end of the pier, Colleens is well placed for those who prefer looking at the sand to sitting on it. A separate kiosk is a children's paradise selling 25 flavours of ice cream.

Highlight: Delicious cakes and casual lunches overlooking Greve de Lecq beach

81

THE HUNGRY MAN

Rozel Pier | 01534 863227

Opening Times: Monday-Sunday 9.30am-4/6pm (closed Mondays during school term; shuts earlier if weather bad or sold out)

Average price two-course à la carte meal for one (excluding drinks): £10

Car Parking: On the road out of Rozel

On the end of the pier in Rozel, The Hungry Man has a mythical status as a place to go the morning after the night before. Sea air and a gentle stroll around the harbour past colourful beach houses and tidy fishermen's cottages, contributes to the cure as much as the actual offerings. The cafe is really a kiosk, brightly painted in a Punch and Judy style, with blackboards displaying the menus and benches lined up along the pier. As well as cream teas with giant scones, Jersey Dairy ice creams and other snacks, there's a good selection of savoury fare too with giant burgers made with Genuine Jersey beef from Brooklands Farm, full breakfasts and, locally caught crab-sandwiches. Particularly busy at weekends or whenever it is sunny, send the fastest member of your party ahead to get in the queue otherwise if you're not a hungry man when you arrive, you certainly will be when you get served.

Highlight: Crab sandwiches and local burgers on the pier

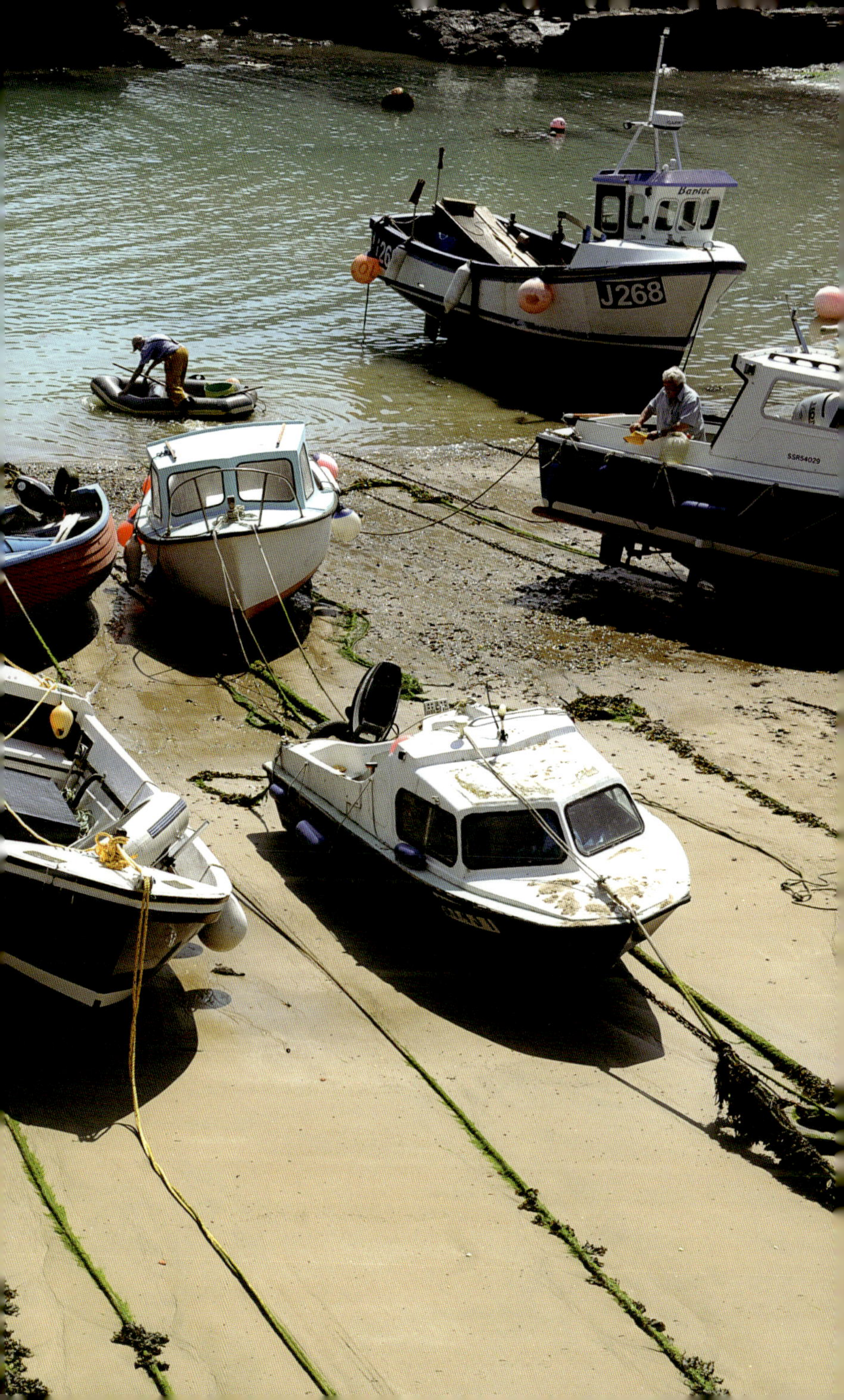
J268
SSR54029

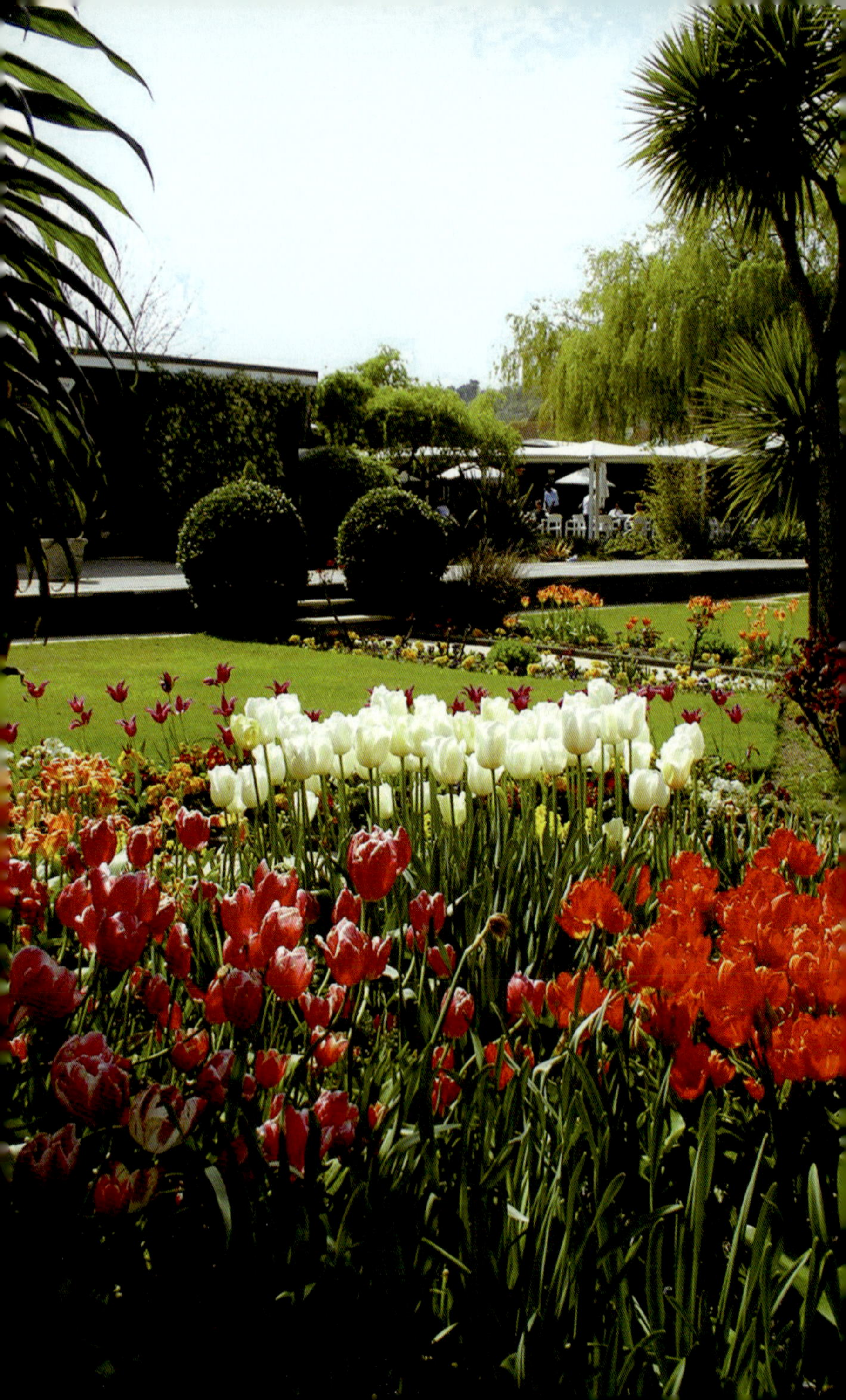

SPINNAKERS

Jersey Pottery, Gorey Village, Grouville, JE3 9EP
01534 850831 | www.jerseypottery.com

Opening Times: Sunday-Thursday 9am-5pm; Friday-Saturday 9am-7pm
Average price two-course à la carte meal for one (excluding drinks): £15
House Wine Bottle: £10.70; **Glass:** £2.60 | **Car Parking:** Large car park on site

Bright and family-friendly, with a lovely garden and play area, Spinnakers is Jersey Pottery's first restaurant. Next to the pottery shop, Spinnakers is set up as a cafeteria, so it's self-service for drinks and cakes, like the crisp treacle tart or giant chocolate fudge cake, but hot food will be delivered to your table. Sandwiches, priced up to £6 and main courses in the £8-10 range, are obviously not cheap; however, as with all Pottery's venues there's an emphasis on quality local produce. The menu offers something for all palates with plenty of salads for summer lunches, grilled meats, fish, pasta, Thai curries and even oysters and lobster for something more sophisticated. The children's menu has typical dishes like spaghetti bolognaise or chicken goujons and chips, alongside healthy choices like steamed salmon with vegetables, or for budding gourmets, a platter of smoked salmon and baby gambas.

Highlight: Family-friendly space with a tempting menu for simple and sophisticated tastes

COCORICO

33 Hillgrove Street, St Helier, JE2 4SL
07700 703919 | www.cocoricojersey.com

Opening Times: Monday-Wednesday 8am-5pm; Thursday-Friday 8am-9pm; Saturday 8am-5pm

Average price two-course à la carte meal for one (excluding drinks): £7

While many places claim to offer a taste of France, few deliver a bite of Brittany. CocoRico is a French embassy for food in the middle of St Helier. Chef/owner Sebastien uses local produce to make his native crêpes, galettes, waffles and quiches along with fresh soups, salads and his special, sourdough bread. Through the window the small cafe resembles an interior design shop with its antique style furniture and gift items for sale, however, the large tables and wooden benches provide a communal space to relax with a delicious cup of coffee and a slice of home-made cake. These range from creamy apricot tarts, fruit basking like golden suns in set custard, to a simple lemon loaf, full of almonds and citrus zest. Using Jersey produce such as cream, butter and eggs, CocoRico's black butter and caramel flavoured macarons come with a Genuine Jersey stamp, although the bright pink raspberry, pale green pistachio and other flavours are just as attractive. At weekends CocoRico makes candyfloss and sets up the crêpe plate outside.

Highlight: Genuine Jersey macarons are the local Ladurée

NOW OPEN

LOCATIONS AND TRAVEL

No matter how small Jersey seems when you first arrive, the longer you spend on the island the further apart everything becomes. After just a few years living here, people who once upon a time might have thought nothing about travelling over an hour to work and back each day start to question driving a couple of miles to another parish. At just nine miles by five, the biggest distance on the island, from St Brelade's to Gorey takes a lot less than an hour even with traffic. Nevertheless, if you are keen to eat in specific restaurants during your time on the island, it is wise to plan your routes so you can maximise what you see. Thankfully, come lunch or dinner time, no matter where you are there is always somewhere good to eat.

JERSEY

- St John
- St Mary
- St Ouen
- St Martin
- St Brelade
- St Aubin
- St Saviour
- St Helier
- St Clement

St Helier

Central: La Capannina, Gio's Restaurant, Restaurant do Porto, Atlantique Seafood Bar, Restaurant de la Poste, Bistro Rosa, CocoRico

Weighbridge: The Royal Yacht Grill, Sirocco, Merchant House Brasserie, Wildfire, Bento, Jaipur

West: The Candlelight, Little Italy, Tassili, La Cantina, The Green Olive

East: Bohemia, Roseville Bistro

St Saviour

Longueville Manor

St Martin

North: Chateau la Chaire, The Hungry Man

Gorey: Suma's, The Bass and Lobster, Feast, Spinnakers, Castle Green

St Clement

Le Hocq Inn, Green Island

St Brelade

The Oyster Box, Crab Shack, The Wayside Cafe, The Beach House

St Ouen

North: Plemont Beach Cafe, North Point Bistro, Colleen's, Le Moulin de Lecq

West: El Tico, Ocean

St Mary

St Mary's Country Inn

St John

Bonne Nuit Beach Cafe

St Aubin

The Boat House, Sails Brasserie, The Salty Dog Bistro, Danny's, The Old Courthouse Inn, Murray's, Tides, Gunsite Cafe

FOOD EVENTS

May – Jersey Food Festival
The inaugural event of spring 2011 featured visits to Genuine Jersey producers, cooking lessons with local chefs and a food fair in St Helier. www.genuinejersey.com

August – Jersey Fish Festival
A celebration of seafood organised by the Jersey Fisherman's Association with food stalls, a water carnival and cooking demonstrations. www.jerseyfishfestival.com

October – La Faîs'si d'Cidre
This traditional cider making at Hamptonne, a 17th century farm, includes horse-powered apple crushing and tastings. www.jerseyheritage.org

Black butter, a spicy apple jam is also made during the autumn at The Elms, the country house head quarters of Jersey National Trust. www.nationaltrustjersey.org.je

November – Tennerfest
Takes place every October/November with most island restaurants offering set menus starting from £10. www.tennerfest.com

For dates and more details on food related events see www.jersey.com

GETTING TO JERSEY

As an island there are two ways of getting to Jersey, by sea or by air.

Condor Ferries run fast daytime services from Poole and Weymouth (journey takes about four hours), and a slow overnight and day ferry from Portsmouth. You can also get to Jersey from Guernsey (one hour) and St Malo (one hour). See www.condorferries.co.uk

For French travellers, or those holidaying in Normandy, there are summer ferries with **Manche Iles Express** from Granville and Carteret (one hour) at times designed to make a day trip to Jersey possible. See www.manche-iles-express.com

Flybe have the largest number of direct routes into Jersey. As well as frequent flights from London Gatwick and Southampton which serve as connecting hubs, there are regular flights from Edinburgh, Doncaster-Sheffield, Birmingham, Cardiff, Exeter, Bristol and Manchester, plus weekly or bi-weekly services from airports including Aberdeen, Inverness, London Luton, Newcastle, Norwich and Belfast City. See **www.flybe.com**

British Airways operate frequent flights from London Gatwick, where you can connect from international or regional services. **www.britishairways.com**

Easyjet run daily flights from Liverpool and summer flights from Glasgow. See **www.easyjet.com**

Jet 2 operate summer flights from Belfast International, Leeds-Bradford and Blackpool. See **www.jet2.com**

Aer Lingus fly from Cork and Dublin in the summer. See www.aerlingus.com

BMI Baby has daily flights from Manchester and Nottingham East Midlands. See **www.bmibaby.com**

Blue Islands go from Bristol, Southampton, Guernsey and London City. **www.blueislands.com**

Aurigny fly from London Stansted and Guernsey. See **www.aurigny.com**

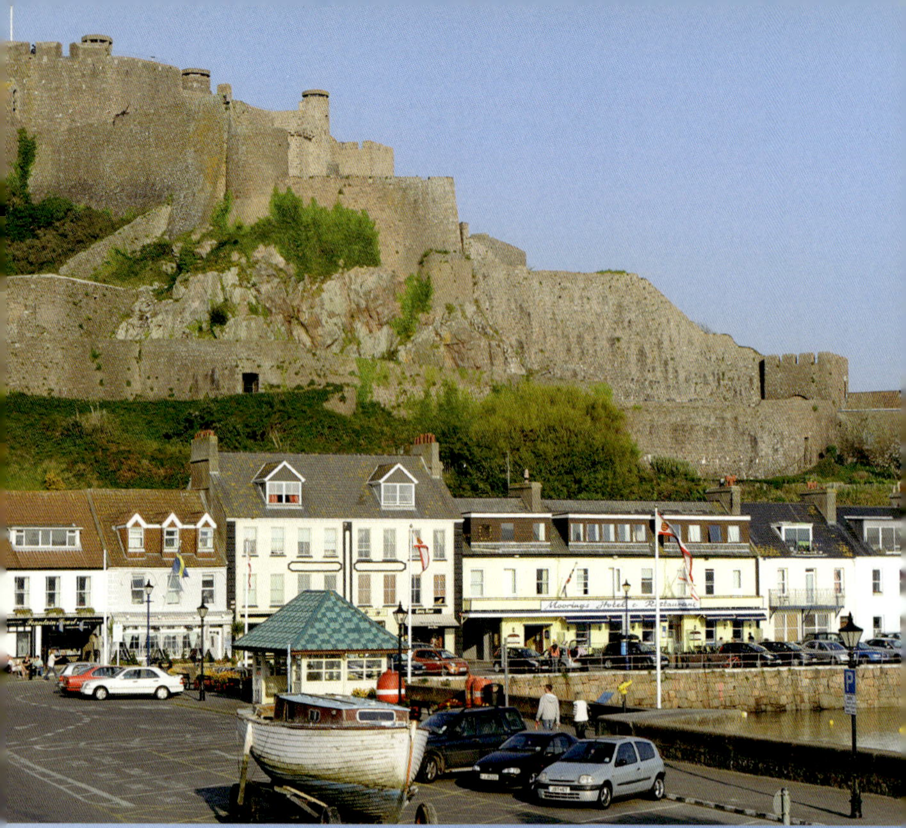
Moorings Hotel & Restaurant

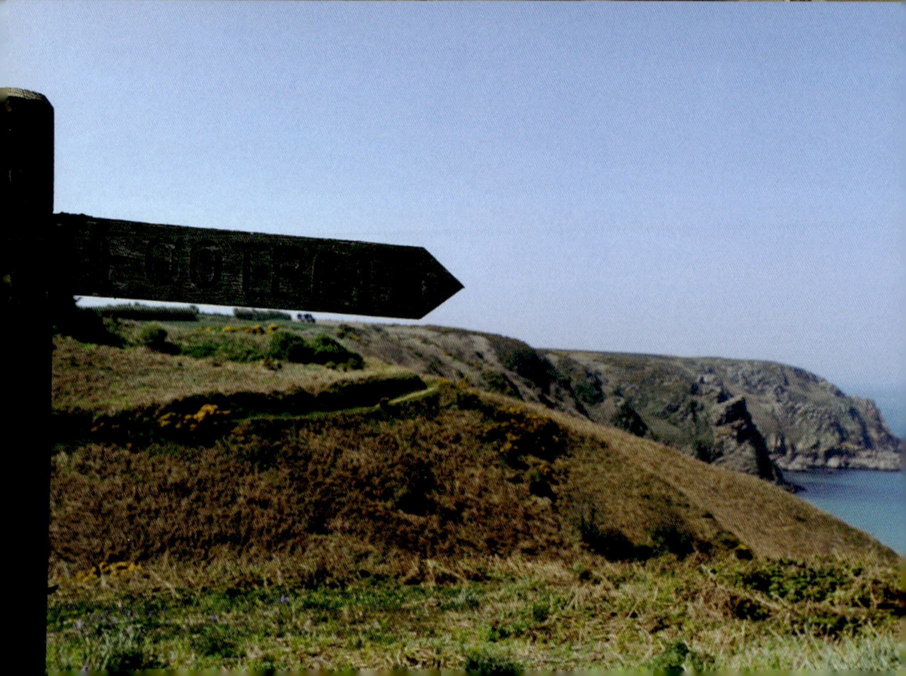

TRAVEL ON THE ISLAND

Do not drink and drive. Jersey has plenty of taxis and car back companies which will drive you home after a good night out. There are taxi ranks at the airport and harbour and in St Helier at Weighbridge, Snow Hill and Library Place. Other services include:

Luxicabs – 01534 887000

Yellow Cabs – 01534 888888

Home James – 01534 630700

Citicabs – 01534 499999

Jersey's buses are run by Connex and all routes start at Liberation Station, St Helier. For timetables see **www.mybus.je**

There are several circular routes which are good for seeing the island during the day as well as a few evening routes e.g. to Gorey. Tickets from £1.10/£1.70. Services can be several hours apart so if you're going to use buses it is worth planning your trip properly.

PHOTOGRAPH CREDITS

The following establishments have supplied images for The Good Taste Guide: Jersey and maintain copyright of those images. All other images by Victoria Stewart.

Bento (interior and food shots)

Bohemia

Longueville Manor

Merchant House Brasserie (interior and food shots)

Sails Brasserie

Sirocco

Tassili Grand Jersey (food shots)

The Somerville Hotel

The Beach House

The Boat House

The Grill (Royal Yacht)

The Oyster Box (food shot)

Crab Shack

Spinnakers

Castle Green

The Atlantic Hotel

La Cantina (food shot)

The Candlelight (interior)

Victoria Stewart is a freelance photographer working for UK newspapers and magazines covering events such as London Fashion Week, The Mobo Awards, sporting fixtures and royal visits. Currently based in Scotland, Victoria also undertakes assignments from corporate clients and runs a successful wedding photography business. For more details visit www.victoriastewartphotography.com and www.marrymepix.co.uk

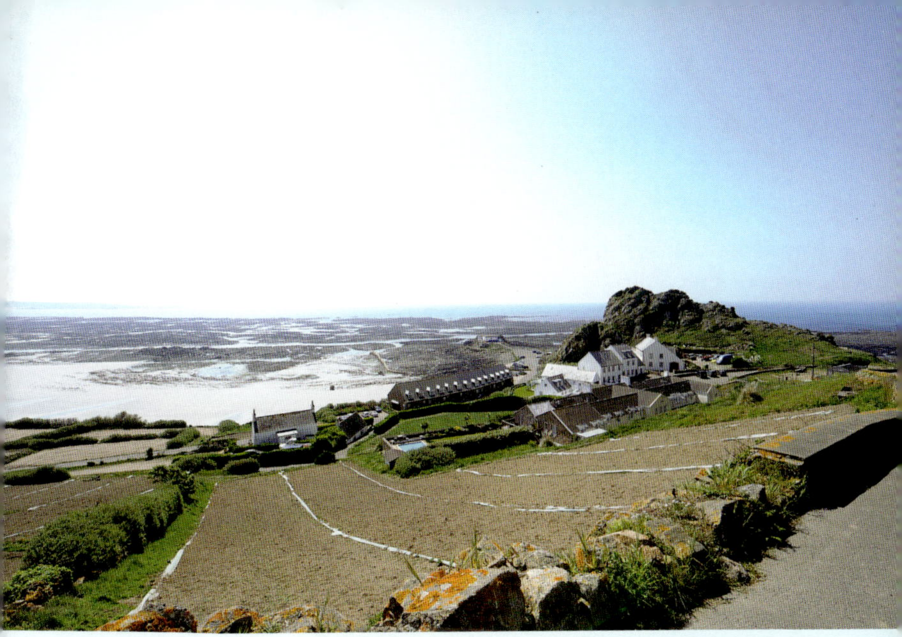

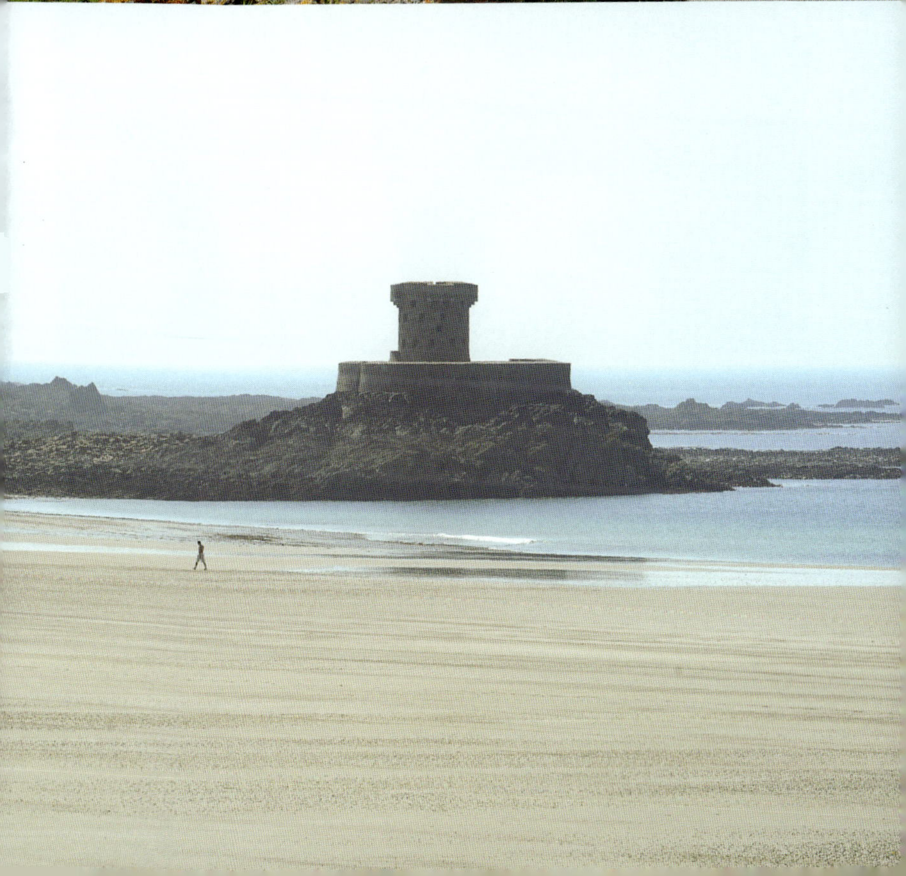

ABOUT THE AUTHOR

Julia Hunt is a freelance journalist living in Jersey. After working in news and features for many years with Scotland's biggest selling newspaper, Julia left to pursue a career in travel writing. She has written for a wide range of national newspapers including The Sunday Mail, The Herald and The Sunday Telegraph, and contributed to UK restaurant guides and international magazines. Since moving to Jersey Julia has developed her interest in food writing and has studied cookery to a professional level at Highlands College, St Helier.